Wuthering Heights

by Emily Brontë

CEFR level B2

Adapted by Karen Kovacs
for
Read Stories – Learn English

Read Stories – Learn English

Wuthering Heights: CEFR level B2 (ELT Graded Reader)
Original text by Emily Brontë
Adapted text © Karen Kovacs, 2025
Logo © Karen Kovacs, 2025

No part of this book may be reproduced, scanned or distributed in any printed or electronic form without permission. Please do not participate in or encourage piracy of copyrighted materials in violation of the author's rights. Thank you for respecting the hard work of the author.

CONTENTS

What are graded readers?   Page 4

Meet the author   Page 5

People in the story   Page 7

The story   Page 9

More stories   Page 148

Get a free story   Page 150

Words from the story   Page 151

WHAT ARE GRADED READERS?

Graded readers are books in easy English. They are written for learners of English and they have **vocabulary and grammar at your level**.

Each book has some new, more difficult words. There are **definitions** for these words at the back of the book.

WHY READ GRADED READERS?

- Studies show that learners who read in English **improve in all areas much more quickly** than learners who don't read.

- With graded readers, you **don't need a dictionary** so reading is more **relaxing**.

- The stories are all in **modern English**.

- You can learn vocabulary and grammar **in context** (this is the best way, according to teachers).

- Reading a book in English will improve your **comprehension**, your **fluency** and your **confidence**.

- The stories are **exciting** and reading them is **fun**!

Meet
the author

My name is Karen.

- I'm the author of many books for English learners.
- I've been nominated 3 times for a Language Learner Literature Award.
- I have a Degree in English Literature and a Master's in Linguistics.
- I'm an experienced English teacher, in the UK and abroad.
- I speak Hungarian, French and Spanish, so I understand how it feels to learn a new language!

Karen Kovacs

ReadStories-LearnEnglish.com

Discover this unforgettable Jane Austen story in a clear, accessible adaptation, also at level B2.

Lose yourself in Anne Elliot's world of love, regret and second chances.

New words

When you see a word in **bold**, go to the back of the book. There you will find a definition of the word.

People in the story

The Earnshaw household
Family home – Wuthering Heights

Catherine Earnshaw (Heathcliff calls her Cathy)
Hindley Earnshaw – Catherine's brother
Frances Earnshaw – Hindley's wife
Hareton Earnshaw – Hindley's son
Heathcliff – an **orphan**
Linton Heathcliff
Nelly Dean – servant
Joseph – servant
Zillah – servant

The Linton household

Family home – Thrushcross Grange

Edgar Linton

Isabella Linton – Edgar's sister

Cathy Linton

Lockwood – a **tenant** at Thrushcross Grange

To see a family tree, as well as a timeline for the story, register for the free materials on my website.

Wuthering Heights

Chapter 1

1801. I've just returned from a visit to my landlord, the only neighbour I will have here. This is certainly a beautiful place. In the whole of England, I don't think I could have chosen anywhere more remote. Perfect if you want to avoid society – and Mr Heathcliff and I are such a suitable pair to share that **solitude**. He's a fantastic guy! He couldn't have imagined how my heart warmed to him when I saw his black eyes look so suspiciously at me, as I rode up and announced my name.

"Mr Heathcliff?" I said.

A nod was the answer.

"Mr Lockwood, your new **tenant**, sir. Please allow me to express the hope that I'm not causing you any trouble by renting Thrushcross Grange. I heard yesterday that you had had some doubts—"

"Thrushcross Grange belongs to me, sir," he interrupted, irritated. "I wouldn't allow anyone to cause me any trouble, if I could prevent it. Come in!"

He said "come in" through closed teeth, as if he really meant, "Go to hell!" This made me decide to accept the invitation because I felt interested in a man who seemed even more **reserved** than myself.

As we entered the **courtyard**, which was in a very poor state, he called out, "Joseph, take Mr Lockwood's horse and bring up some wine."

Jospeh was an elderly man, though strong and healthy. He looked at me sourly as he took my horse from me and muttered something to himself.

Wuthering Heights is the name of Mr Heathcliff's home. "Wuthering" is a local word that describes the strong winds and storms the house is exposed to in bad weather. And you can tell how fierce the north winds are by the **fir trees** at the end of the house: they lean heavily to one side. Luckily, the architect designed the house to be strong: it is built from rough stone and the narrow windows are set deep into the walls.

Before I stepped inside, I looked up and saw the date "1500" in stone above the door along with the name "Hareton Earnshaw". I would have asked the **grumpy** owner about the history of the place but I saw that he wanted me either to come in quickly or leave entirely so and I decided not to bother him.

We walked straight into the family sitting room – there is no entrance hall. I noticed a huge **fireplace** but no sign of roasting, boiling or baking so it was clear the kitchen must be deeper inside the house.

Above the chimney, there were several big old guns. The floor was smooth, white stone and the chairs had high backs and were painted green. Under a piece of furniture in a dark corner, there was a brown dog surrounded by puppies, and other dogs haunted other corners.

This room and its furniture would have suited a northern farmer perfectly, the kind that is common in these hills. But Mr Heathcliff forms a **sharp contrast** to this house and way of life. He's dark-skinned and looks pretty **slovenly**, yet he behaves like a gentleman. He has a handsome, upright figure.

I took a seat by the fireplace and, as my landlord remained silent for a while, I started to stroke the dog, who had left her puppies and moved to the back of my legs. As my hand touched her fur, she **growled** and tried to bite me.

"You'd better leave the dog alone," growled Mr Heathcliff also, giving it a kick as he spoke. "We don't keep her as a pet." Then he walked over to a side door and called out, "Joseph!"

Joseph mumbled something from the cellar but showed no sign of coming up so his master went down to him, leaving me face to face with the aggressive dog. I sat still but stared at her. Unfortunately, this was enough to make her furious and she suddenly jumped onto my knees. I pushed her back but then half a dozen other dogs emerged from various hiding places and tried to attack me. I had to call for help.

A servant ran from the kitchen with a frying pan in her hand and started hitting the dogs with it. This calmed them down.

Meanwhile, Mr Heathcliff came back into the room. "What the hell is the matter?" he asked angrily.

"Your crazy dogs were attacking me!" I muttered.

"They were only defending the property. They're not used to guests," he remarked, putting a bottle down in front of me. "A glass of wine?"

We sat down together and had an interesting conversation about the local area. I found him very intelligent and, before I went home, I suggested that I visit him again tomorrow. It was obvious he didn't want that but I'll go anyway.

Yesterday afternoon was misty and cold. After a four-mile walk, I arrived at Heathcliff's **bleak** house just as snow started to fall.

I knocked loudly on the door. Joseph popped his head

out of the round window of a farm building.

"What do you want?" he shouted. "The master's in the fields with the sheep." His head vanished again, without waiting for an answer.

Then I saw a young man in the courtyard and he indicated for me to follow him. Soon, I was back in the same huge, warm room as before. A massive fire was burning brightly and lunch was already on the table.

Sat at the table, there was a woman. I waited for her to invite me to sit down but she just looked at me in silence.

"Terrible weather!" I remarked.

She didn't open her mouth but she kept her eyes on me, an unfriendly expression on her face.

"Sit down," the young man said **gruffly**. "He'll be in soon."

I obeyed.

"You shouldn't have come," said my hostess, standing up to get something. I had a good view of her figure now. She was slim, with the most beautiful face I'd ever seen and curly golden hair.

Getting some cups, she demanded, "Were you asked to tea?"

"I would love a cup," I answered.

"Were you asked?" she repeated.

"No," I said.

Meanwhile, the young man stood in front of the fire, looking down at me as if I were his enemy. Was he a servant or not? I wasn't sure. He was certainly not as sophisticated as Mr and Mrs Heathcliff but he wasn't serving the lady of the house.

I was relieved when Heathcliff finally came in.

"Why did you choose to come here during a snow storm?" he said. "You could have been lost forever." Then he turned to the lady. "Make the tea!" He said it so aggressively that I jumped. I was beginning to think he wasn't such a fantastic guy after all.

We all sat down to drink our tea.

After a minute's awkward silence, I said, "I'm pleased to meet your wife, Mr Heathcliff."

"My wife!" he answered, an unpleasant smile on his face.

I knew then I had made a mistake. It's true she's too young to be his wife – he looked about forty and she was more like seventeen.

Then I realised, "Ah, that rough man who's eating his bread with unwashed hands might be her husband, and Heathcliff's son. She hardly sees anyone in this remote place or she would never have chosen someone like him!"

I don't want to sound arrogant but he really was disgusting, whereas I'm fairly attractive.

"Mrs Heathcliff is my daughter-in-law," said Heathcliff, confirming my conclusion.

"Yes, I see," I remarked, turning to the young man. "You're the lucky husband of this delightful lady."

This was worse than before. He went red and looked like he wanted to punch me.

"Neither of us are married to her," Heathcliff explained. "Her husband's dead. He was my son."

"And this young man is …"

"Not my son." Heathcliff smiled his unpleasant smile again.

"My name is Hareton Earnshaw," growled the other man, "and I advise you to respect it."

I nearly laughed at this ridiculous warning but he was staring angrily at me so I stopped myself.

When we'd finished eating, I approached a window to see what the weather was like. It was already getting dark and the sky and hills were covered in snow.

"I don't think it'll be possible for me to get home now without a guide," I admitted. "The roads will be buried and I'll get lost. What shall I do?"

There was no reply to my question.

Joseph came in, bringing some food for the dogs, and saw Mrs Heathcliff sat down. "How can you sit there, lazy girl, when everyone else is working? You'll go to the devil, like your mother did."

"Stop threatening me, old man," she replied, "or I'll ask the devil to come and take you away, as a special favour to me!"

He hurried out, praying.

Mrs Heathcliff and I found ourselves alone for a moment. I turned to her and said, "With that face, I'm sure you must be good-hearted. Please tell me, can I stay the night?"

"Ask your host," she answered coldly. "It's got nothing to do with me."

"I hope this teaches you to think before making a journey on these hills in bad weather," Heathcliff's **harsh** voice called from the kitchen.

I was fed up now. I went outside, grabbed a lamp from Joseph, who was milking the cows, and rushed towards the gate.

"Master, he's stealing the lamp!" shouted the old man. "Gnasher! Fang! Get him!"

As I reached the gate, two hairy dogs jumped at my throat, knocking me to the ground and putting out the light, while Heathcliff and Hareton stood laughing. Luckily, the dogs quickly lost interest in me but I ended up with a nosebleed anyway.

The female servant, Zillah, rushed out, crying, "Poor man. He can hardly breathe!"

With that, she threw a jug of icy water down my neck and pulled me into the kitchen.

Feeling sick and dizzy, I had no choice but to stay under Heathcliff's roof after all.

Chapter 2

While leading me upstairs to bed, Zillah suggested that I should hide the candle and not make a noise because her master had strange ideas about the bedroom she was putting me in. He never let anybody stay in there willingly but she didn't know why as she'd only been in the house a year or two.

Too tired to be curious, I closed my door and got into bed. The window **ledge** where I put my candle down had a few old books piled up in one corner and it was covered with writing scratched into the paint. The writing was a name repeated, large and small: *Catherine Earnshaw*, here and there varied to *Catherine Heathcliff*, and then again to *Catherine Linton*.

I leant my head against the window and continued spelling *Catherine Earnshaw*, *Heathcliff*, *Linton* in my head, till my eyes closed. Soon, white letters rose up in the dark before me, as vivid as ghosts. The air was filled with Catherines.

I sat up, rubbed my eyes and grabbed a book from the ledge. I examined it and then picked up another. I soon saw that every blank space was covered in childish writing, which seemed a kind of diary.

I began to read the faded handwriting. "An awful Sunday," I read. "I wish my father was still here. Hindley's a rubbish substitute. He treats Heathcliff terribly. H and I are going to rebel. We took the first step this evening.

"It had been raining all day so we couldn't go to church. Instead, we went up into the attic and Joseph read to us from the Bible. While Hindley and his wife warmed themselves by the fire downstairs, Heathcliff and I sat shivering, listening to Joseph. We thought he'd be quick because he must have been cold too. But no! The service lasted three hours!

"We finally went back downstairs and started playing quietly, as we used to be allowed to do on Sundays, but Hindley told us off.

"'Have you forgotten that you've got a new master?'" shouted the **tyrant**. 'I'll beat you if you annoy me again! Be quiet.'

"Joseph brought us some 'good, moral books' but mine was so boring that I couldn't bear reading it so I threw it out the window. 'I hate moral books!' I shouted. Heathcliff kicked his and tore the cover.

"The old man started shouting at us – 'The devil's going

to come for you!' – and Hindley hurried from his heaven by the fireplace, seized us both by the collar and threw us into the storage room. I reached for this book and started writing in it. Heathcliff is getting bored though and says we should escape, and go and play on the **moors**. It's a good idea and, if Joseph comes to look for us and finds us missing, he might think his prediction has come true!"

A later entry read: "I never dreamt that Hindley could make me cry this much! Poor Heathcliff! Hindley won't let him sit with us or eat with us anymore, and he says I can't play with H or he'll send him away. He blames father and says he **spoilt** H."

My eyes grew tired and soon I fell asleep. But I had such a terrible night! I don't remember a worse one.

I had a nightmare that I was at church. The priest had been talking for several hours when, suddenly, he declared to everyone that I was a **sinner**. Everyone rushed at me and started beating me, including Joseph, who hit me harder than anyone. The priest stood at the front, banging his hand on a wooden ledge in front of him. It was so loud that it woke me up.

Actually, the noise was coming from the branch of a fir tree that hit my window every time the wind blew.

I fell asleep and dreamt again. I heard the strong wind,

the snow falling heavily to the ground and the tree repeating its sound. It annoyed me so much that I got up and tried to open the window but couldn't. I smashed my hand against the glass, breaking it, and stretched my arm out to seize the irritating branch. Instead, my fingers grabbed the fingers of a little, ice-cold hand!

A feeling of horror took control of me. I tried to pull my arm back but the hand **clung** to it and a melancholy voice sobbed, "Let me in! Let me in!"

"Who are you?" I asked, struggling, meanwhile, to release my arm.

"Catherine Linton," it replied, the voice shivering (why did I think of *Linton*? I had read *Earnshaw* twenty times for Linton). "I've come home. I'd lost my way on the moor!"

As it spoke, I could just make out a child's face looking through the window. Terror made me cruel. The creature was still clinging to my arm, so I pulled its wrist onto the broken glass, rubbing it backwards and forwards until the blood ran down onto the bed sheets. Still, it sobbed, "Let me in!" I was almost mad with fear.

"How can I?" I said. "Let *me* go, if you want me to let you in!"

The fingers relaxed. I pulled mine through the hole and hurriedly piled the books up against it.

The cry continued for a quarter of an hour.

"Go away!" I shouted finally. "I'll never let you in, not if you beg for twenty years."

"It *is* twenty years," cried the melancholy voice. "I've been an **outcast** for twenty years!"

At that moment, there was a faint scratching noise outside and the pile of books moved as if someone was pushing them forwards.

I tried to jump up but I couldn't move so I yelled aloud, panicked and terrified.

My yelling caused someone to rush towards my bedroom door and push it open with a strong hand. I sat trembling and wiping the sweat from my forehead.

It was Heathcliff. He didn't see me at first. "At last," he said in a half-whisper.

Then I moved and he **started**, his face as white as the wall behind him.

"It's only your guest, sir," I called out. "I had a nightmare and screamed in my sleep. Sorry I disturbed you."

"Damn you, Mr Lockwood!" he said. "Who put you in this room?"

"It was your servant Zillah," I replied, "and I wish she hadn't. This place is haunted! That Catherine Linton, or

Earnshaw, or whatever her name was – she must have been a little devil! She told me she'd been walking the earth for the past twenty years: a punishment for her many sins, I bet!"

I'd hardly spoken these words before I remembered the connection between Heathcliff's and Catherine's names in the book and I blushed.

"**How dare you** talk to me like that under my own roof?" shouted Heathcliff, striking his forehead with rage.

It was only three o'clock in the morning but, not wanting to stay any longer, I told Heathcliff I'd leave as soon as it was daylight.

I started walking out the room but turned back just in time to see him do something very strange. He forced open the window, bursting into tears as he did it. "Come in!" he sobbed. "Cathy, my darling! Hear me *this* time, Cathy!"

Ghosts don't tend to appear when asked, and this one was no different. But the snow and wind blew wildly through, even blowing out my candle.

I left my landlord to his shouts of grief, not understanding what caused them exactly, and went downstairs.

As soon as I could, I escaped the house. I got lost several times because the moors were like a white ocean and anything familiar was covered in snow. But, after four hours, I eventually arrived back at Thrushcross Grange.

One of the servants, who had been worried about me, brought me a steaming cup of coffee.

Chapter 3

What strange creatures we are! I'd been fully determined to avoid all social interaction (after all, I was in the perfect place for that!) but, before long, I found myself struggling with the solitude. That's why, when Mrs Dean brought in my dinner, I asked her to sit with me while I ate.

"You've lived at Thrushcross Grange quite a while," I began.

"Eighteen years, sir. I came when the mistress was married. After she died, the master kept me as his **housekeeper**."

"I see."

There was a brief silence. I began to wonder if she was one of those people who didn't gossip. But then, after a minute or so, she cried out, "Oh, times have changed massively since then!"

"I'm sure they have," I remarked encouragingly.

I wanted to turn the conversation to my landlord's family, and that pretty widow girl – I was keen to know her story. With that in mind, I asked Mrs Dean why Heathcliff rented out Thrushcross Grange and preferred living in a house that was in a worse state.

"Well, he's rich so money isn't the problem!" she answered. "But he didn't want to turn down a paying tenant. It's strange some people are so greedy, when they're alone in the world!"

"He had a son, is that right?"

"Yes, but he's dead."

"And that young lady, Mrs Heathcliff, is his widow?"

"Yes."

"Where did she come from originally?"

"She's my **late** master's daughter: Catherine Linton was her **maiden name**. I looked after her when she was a baby, poor thing!"

"What? Catherine Linton?" I cried, astonished. But I quickly realised it wasn't my ghostly Catherine. "So a man called Mr Linton lived here before me?" I asked.

"Yes."

"And who's that young man, Hareton Earnshaw, who lives with Mr Heathcliff? Are they related?"

"No. He's the late Mrs Linton's nephew."

"The young lady's cousin, then?" I asked.

"Yes. And her husband was her cousin as well: one on the mother's, the other on the father's side. Heathcliff married Mr Linton's sister."

"I see the house at Wuthering Heights has 'Earnshaw' over the front door. Are they an old family?"

"Very old, sir," said Mrs Dean. "And Hareton's the last of them, as our Miss Cathy is of us – I mean, of the Lintons. Have you been to Wuthering Heights? Excuse the question but I'd like to hear how she is!"

"Mrs Heathcliff? She looked very well and beautiful, but not very happy."

"Oh dear!" Mrs Dean replied. "But I'm not surprised. And did you like the master?"

"He's very rough."

"Rough and hard as stone!" the housekeeper agreed. "Stay away from him, if you can."

"He must have had a tough life to make him so grumpy," I remarked. "Do you know anything about him?"

"I know everything about him, except where he was born, and who were his parents, and how he made his money. Hareton's been treated so badly! The poor boy is the only one around here who doesn't know he's been deceived."

"Mrs Dean," I said, "will you sit and chat to me for an hour? I'd like to hear more."

"Of course, sir!" she answered, pleased to find me so sociable. "Let me just get my sewing. And you've caught a cold – I heard you sneezing. I'll bring you a hot drink."

I moved nearer the fire. She was right – I wasn't well. She came back and started her story.

* * * * *

Before I came to live here (she began), I was almost always at Wuthering Heights because my mother had looked after Mr Hindley Earnshaw when he was a child, that was Hareton's father, and I used to play with the children and do little tasks.

When Miss Catherine was six years old and Hindley fourteen, their father Mr Earnshaw went to Liverpool on business. After three long days, he finally returned, at eleven o'clock at night. The children had refused to go to sleep and were waiting for him.

They rushed at him enthusiastically but stopped when they saw he wasn't alone. There was a dirty, black-haired child with him, about Catherine's age. He just stared at everyone, speaking words none of us understood. I was frightened and Mrs Earnshaw was ready to throw him out.

"What do you want to do with it?" she shouted. "Are you mad bringing home an outcast?"

Her husband explained that he'd found the child on the streets of Liverpool. Not a soul knew who it belonged to and he hadn't wanted to leave it there.

This was Heathcliff's introduction to the family. They named him Heathcliff, and it's been his name ever since, both his first name and surname. He and Catherine became very close but Hindley hated him.

Heathcliff never cried when Hindley punched him, which he often did. But it was hardness, not gentleness, that made him patient.

Mr Earnshaw was furious at Hindley's treatment of the **orphan**, who had quickly become the old master's favourite.

So, you see, from the very beginning, Heathcliff caused bad feeling in the house. And by the time of Mrs Earnshaw's death two years later, Hindley had grown bitter against Heathcliff for replacing him in his father's affections.

It's true that Mr Earnshaw always took Heathcliff's side but then he generally told the truth and never complained. The result was that Heathcliff became incredibly spoilt.

Mr Earnshaw had always been active and healthy but one day he became suddenly unwell. To give him some peace, Hindley was sent away to school.

Catherine was too **unruly** to be anyone's favourite. She was the prettiest girl in the neighbourhood and had the sweetest smile but she was so naughty. She wanted everyone's attention, often spoke very harshly and was constantly teasing Joseph for his religious seriousness. "You'll go to the devil, miss!" he would always warn her, but she would just laugh.

She was much too fond of Heathcliff. The greatest punishment we could invent for her was to keep her separate from him. And Heathcliff would do anything for her.

The hour came, at last, that ended Mr Earnshaw's troubles on earth. He died quietly in his chair one October evening, sat by the fireplace. A strong wind blew round the house and down the chimney.

Catherine only noticed when she went to kiss him good night. "Oh, he's dead, Heathcliff! He's dead!" And they both burst into tears.

I sobbed too but Joseph told us we should be ashamed of ourselves for crying that the master was in heaven.

Catherine and Heathcliff found it hard to sleep that night. It was after midnight when I walked past their half-open bedroom door and heard them **comforting** each other, whispering about how beautiful heaven must be.

Chapter 4

When Hindley came home for his father's funeral, he brought a wife with him. We were astonished. He told us her name, Frances, but nothing else about her.

She was a silly creature but harmless. She was obsessed with the idea of dying. It terrified her but I didn't think she was any more likely to die than I was. She was rather thin but she was young and her eyes sparkled as bright as diamonds. It's true, though, that climbing the stairs did make her quite out of breath.

Hindley Earnshaw had altered considerably in the three years of his absence. On the day of his return, he told Joseph and me to stay in the kitchen and leave the rest of the house to him and his wife.

He was the new master of the house and he soon became **tyrannical**. His old bitterness against Heathcliff returned and he ordered him to eat with the servants and work in the fields. His education, which consisted of lessons from the priest, was stopped immediately.

Heathcliff bore his **degradation** pretty well at first because Catherine taught him what she learnt, and worked or played with him in the fields. They were growing up like **savages** and Hindley didn't care at all. It was only thanks to Joseph that they went to church.

One of their chief amusements was running away to the moors in the morning and staying there all day. The priest was angry with Catherine for missing her lessons and Joseph beat Heathcliff till his arm ached, but they forgot everything the minute they were together again.

One Sunday evening, they were very late home and Hindley told me to lock up the house. "They can sleep on the moors!" he growled.

The household went to bed but I stayed awake, determined to let them in when they finally returned. Eventually, I spotted Heathcliff coming through the gate in the pouring rain.

I opened the door for him. "Where's Miss Catherine?" I cried. "No accident, I hope?"

"She's at Thrushcross Grange," he answered.

"What **on earth** were you doing there?" I asked.

He changed out of his wet clothes and then explained everything.

"Cathy and I were curious to see how the Lintons spent their Sunday evenings," he began, "so we ran all the way to Thrushcross Grange without stopping. And Nelly, we saw that they don't sit shivering in corners while a gruff old servant reads to them for hours from the Bible. No!

"Their curtains were only half closed so we held on to the window ledge and looked in. And Nelly, it was beautiful! There were red carpets, loads of pretty candles and a pure white ceiling bordered in gold. Old Mr and Mrs Linton weren't there – Edgar and his sister were completely alone. They should have been happy, shouldn't they? We would have felt we were in heaven.

"But guess what they were doing! Isabella, who's about eleven, a year younger than Cathy, lay screaming at the far end of the room as if someone was stabbing her, and Edgar stood by the fireplace crying silently. They'd obviously been arguing over something. We laughed at the spoilt **brats**! I wouldn't change places with them for anything, even if I could throw Joseph off the roof and paint the house with Hindley's blood!"

"Don't talk like that!" I interrupted. "And you still haven't told me why Catherine hasn't come back with you."

"I told you we laughed," he answered. "The Lintons heard us and shot like arrows to the door. They started shouting for their parents, and we made scary noises to frighten them even more! Then we heard an adult coming so we started to run away but Cathy fell. 'Run, Heathcliff!'

she whispered. 'They've let the guard-dog loose, and he's got me!' The devil had seized her ankle, Nelly! But she was too brave to yell!

"I grabbed a stone and put it between the dog's jaws, then I tried to push it down the **beast**'s throat. A servant came a minute later and took the dog away, then he came back for us and took us inside.

"'You were trying to burgle the house, I bet,' old Mr Linton said to me, 'and then murder us in our sleep.' He turned to his wife. 'Look at that dirty thief, Mary. He should be hanged.'

"The cowardly children moved nearer to us, Isabella complaining, 'Horrible thing! Put him in the cellar, Father.'

"Cathy laughed at this and they all looked at her. 'That's Miss Earnshaw!' Edgar whispered to his mother. He recognised her from church although they'd never spoken. 'Look, Skulker has bitten her foot – it's bleeding!'

"Mrs Linton was shocked by this and Mr Linton remarked, 'Her brother's very careless with her, allowing her to run around on the moors with this foreign outcast!'

"I started swearing at them – don't be angry, Nelly – and they threw me outside and locked the door. When I looked in through the window, Cathy was sat on the sofa and a servant was washing her feet. Edgar couldn't keep his blue eyes from her face and Isabella was combing her hair.

"So I left her there. She was happy with them, after all."

Catherine stayed at Thrushcross Grange for five weeks, until Christmas (continued Mrs Dean). By that time, her ankle was thoroughly cured and her manners much improved. Instead of a wild savage running in to hug me, a sophisticated young lady entered the house. She kissed me gently. The dogs rushed to greet her but she hardly dared touch them as she didn't want to ruin her beautiful silk dress.

Then she looked for Heathcliff but he was hiding behind the sofa. Since Catherine had been gone, nobody except me had taken any care of him so he was even dirtier than ever.

"Heathcliff, come out and welcome Catherine home, like the other servants," ordered Hindley.

But Catherine spotted him first and flew to him, covering him in kisses. Laughing, she cried, "Oh, Heathcliff, you do look angry and moody! And dirty! But that's because I'm used to Edgar and Isabella Linton now. Well, Heathcliff, have you forgotten me?"

It wasn't a stupid question because embarrassment and pride made his expression even darker than usual and he refused to even move.

"What's wrong?" she asked him.

"You laughed at me," he replied, **sulking**.

"I couldn't help it," she said. "You look so funny. Don't sulk. If you wash your face and brush your hair, it'll be alright."

"I like being dirty!" he shouted and he ran out of the room.

I went to the kitchen and amused myself by singing Christmas songs while I did the cleaning. But then I remembered how Mr Earnshaw, that kind old man, had been so fond of Heathcliff and had worried he would be badly treated after his death, and I started to cry.

My feelings of guilt made me go and look for the poor orphan. I found him outside. "Heathcliff, come back into the house. Let me dress you smart and then you can go and sit with Miss Catherine and chat until bedtime."

He stubbornly ignored me so I went back into the house.

The next morning, however, when the family were at church, he came to me and said, "Nelly, make me decent. I want to be good."

"The Lintons are coming for lunch," I informed him. "You'll present such a sharp contrast to Edgar once I've tidied you up! He'll look like a doll compared to you. You're taller and twice as broad across the shoulders. You could easily knock him over, don't you think?"

Heathcliff's face **brightened** for a moment but then it grew dark again. "But Nelly, even if I knocked him over twenty times, it wouldn't make him less handsome. I wish I had light hair and fair skin, and was well behaved like him, and had a chance of being as rich as he'll be!"

"And cried for no reason all the time," I added, "and trembled if a country boy raised his **fist** against you, and sat at home all day because there was a drop of rain. Come on, Heathcliff, cheer up!"

After I washed and dressed him, I made him look in the mirror. "Look!" I said proudly. "You're really handsome now, like a prince in disguise! Maybe your father was Emperor of China and your mother an Indian queen. Perhaps you were stolen by evil sailors and brought to England. You should believe it – the thought will give you courage to bear your degradation by that silly little farmer!"

My words gradually improved his mood and he stopped sulking.

The guests arrived and Hindley showed them into the house. Unfortunately, as soon as he saw Heathcliff, Hindley started insulting him.

"Look at your neat, curly hair!" he laughed. "Are you trying to show off? If I pull it, do you think your hair will get even longer?"

"It's long enough already," commented Edgar Linton. "It's hanging over his eyes!"

I don't think he meant to be rude but Heathcliff's violent nature wouldn't allow him to put up with remarks like that. Reaching towards the table, which was prepared for lunch, he seized a dish of hot apple sauce and threw the contents at Edgar's face.

Hindley immediately dragged Heathcliff upstairs.

Catherine was angry with Edgar. "Why did you talk to him? Now Hindley's going to beat him and I'll be too stressed to eat my lunch."

"I didn't!" sobbed the young man. "I promised mother that I wouldn't say one word to him, and I didn't."

I secretly went up later to take him some dinner. When I asked him how he was, he answered seriously, "I'm trying to work out how to get revenge on Hindley. I don't care how long it takes but I must get revenge on him one day. While I'm planning, I don't feel any pain."

Sorry, Mr Lockwood! I should stop talking. It's late and you must be tired.

* * * * *

The housekeeper put down her sewing and got up.

"I'm not tired, Mrs Dean," I insisted. "Please carry on with your story. Except for your regional accent, you don't speak like a servant and I'm enjoying listening to you."

She laughed. "Well, I've always read books from the family's library in my spare time," she explained. "Anyway, I'll continue my story, but I'll pass to the next summer, the summer of 1778, that's nearly twenty-three years ago."

Chapter 5

On the morning of a fine June day, my little darling was born, the last of the ancient Earnshaw stock. We were working in the fields when a servant girl came to announce it to us.

"Such a gorgeous boy!" she said, out of breath from running. "But the doctor says Mrs Earnshaw will be dead before winter. He says she's had tuberculosis these past months. You'll have to take care of it, Nelly. It will be all yours when Mrs Earnshaw's gone!"

I rushed home to admire the boy but I was very sad for Hindley's sake. He **doted on** his wife and I couldn't imagine how he would bear the loss.

As predicted, Frances Earnshaw soon died and the child Hareton was given to me to look after. It was enough for Hindley to know he was healthy and never to hear him cry. He didn't care about him apart from that because he was so **distraught** over his wife.

Hindley got into the habit of drinking and swearing. The other servants wouldn't put up with it and soon only Joseph and I were left.

Hindley was tyrannical towards Heathcliff and, as a result, Heathcliff became crueller. He took pleasure in witnessing his enemy Hindley's degradation. What a savage house we had! The priest stopped coming and nobody decent ever visited, except Edgar Linton.

At fifteen, Catherine was the queen of the countryside – there was no one more beautiful. And she turned out to be an arrogant, **headstrong** creature! I admit I didn't like her.

I often spoke to her impatiently but she never disliked me for it. She was incredibly loyal to those she cared about. She continued to dote on Heathcliff, and even though young Linton seemed the better man, he struggled to make such a deep impression.

Young Linton was my late master: that's his portrait over the fireplace. It used to hang on one side and his wife's on the other, but hers has been removed.

(Mrs Dean raised the candle, and I made out a soft-featured face, very similar to the young lady at Wuthering Heights, but gentler and more thoughtful in expression. He had long fair hair and eyes that were large and serious. The figure was almost too delicate, and it lacked energy.)

Catherine kept seeing the Lintons after her five-week stay with them. She could be charming, and she easily gained the admiration of Isabella and the heart and soul of her brother. She developed a double character, without exactly intending to deceive anyone. At Thrushcross Grange, where she heard Heathcliff called a "savage" and a "beast", she was careful not to act like him. She was full of ambition and she wanted the Lintons to like her. But at home, she had no reason to be polite or control her unruly nature when her efforts would only be laughed at.

Edgar was scared of coming to Wuthering Heights and encountering Hindley. And Catherine wasn't keen for her two friends to meet at all. After all, Edgar and Heathcliff hated each other.

Heathcliff was now sixteen and had by that time lost the benefit of his early education and any love of books. His former sense of **superiority** (from being old Earnshaw's favourite) had completely faded away.

The **deterioration** of his mind was reflected in the deterioration of his appearance. He looked increasingly slovenly and his naturally reserved nature became more extreme. He and Catherine were still constant companions but he'd ceased expressing his fondness for her in words. And when she tried to hug him, he pulled away, knowing there was no point – she was too good for him now.

"Edgar Linton's coming for tea this afternoon," Catherine announced one day.

"You prefer that silly brat to me!" Heathcliff complained sulkily.

"No, I don't," argued Catherine.

"Look at the calendar on the wall," Heathcliff said. "The crosses are for the evenings you've spent with the Lintons, the dots for the evenings spent with me. Do you see?"

"What a waste of time, marking the calendar like that!" cried Catherine impatiently. "And anyway, why should I always be with you? It's not interesting when people know nothing and say nothing."

"You never told me before that I didn't talk enough, Cathy!" Heathcliff said, very upset.

A moment later, Edgar arrived so the friends' conversation ended. As one friend came in and the other went out, the sharp contrast between them was obvious. One was like a bleak, stormy moor and the other like a beautiful, green valley. Edgar had a sweet way of speaking and pronounced his words like you do: less gruff than we talk here and softer.

They started chatting but, before long, Catherine looked up at me angrily. "What are you still doing here, Nelly?" I knew she was still annoyed after her disagreement with Heathcliff.

Hindley had asked me not to leave the two of them alone

so I ignored her and continued cleaning. She walked up to me and said harshly, "Get out, now!"

"No!" I replied.

Then she **slapped** me and I screamed.

"Catherine, love! Catherine!" cried Edgar, greatly shocked at her unexpected violence.

He got up to leave but Catherine went to the door and **grasped** the handle firmly. "No, Edgar Linton," the headstrong girl said. "Sit back down. If you leave, I'll be miserable all night and I won't be miserable for you!"

He was already crazy about her so he wasn't difficult to convince. And instead of being put off by her terrible behaviour, he soon loved her more than ever. "No one can save him," I thought. "He's **doomed**."

Chapter 6

A while later, Hindley came home, swearing and shouting. Little Hareton, who followed me everywhere, was at my feet.

His father grabbed him. "Who's this ugly beast?" he shouted. "It can't be Hareton because, if it was, he would have run to greet his father." The child began sobbing from fear. "Shh, boy, shh. Give me a kiss. What? You won't? Then I'll break your neck!"

In a rage, Hindley carried his son upstairs. I rushed after them, desperate to rescue Hareton, but I was too late. Hindley had leant over the **banister** to listen to a noise from below, almost forgetting what was in his hands. "Who's there?" he demanded, hearing footsteps at the bottom of the stairs.

Hareton, struggling to escape from his father's careless grasp, suddenly freed himself and fell.

There was barely time for me to feel terrified before we saw the boy was safe. Heathcliff had arrived under the banister just at the critical moment and, without thinking, caught him.

As Heathcliff looked up at Hindley, I could clearly see the disappointment on his face. He knew that, in saving his enemy's son, he'd destroyed his chance for revenge. No doubt he was tempted to smash Hareton's head against the steps but he knew we were there to stop him so he didn't attempt it.

"That was your fault, Nelly," Hindley accused me. "You should have kept the boy **out of my sight**."

He grabbed a bottle of brandy from a shelf and poured himself a glass.

"It's a pity he can't kill himself with drink," Heathcliff muttered.

I went into the kitchen and Heathcliff walked out of the house – or so I thought. It turned out that he'd stayed in the room, hidden on the other side of the sofa, as I later found out.

I sat by the fire with Hareton on my lap, singing him a sweet song, when Miss Catherine came in.

"Are you alone, Nelly?" she asked.

"Yes, Miss," I replied.

"Where's Heathcliff?" she said.

"Outside," was my answer.

He didn't correct me. Perhaps he'd **dozed off**.

I glanced up at Catherine and noticed a tear running

down her cheek. "I'm so unhappy!" she cried.

"You're hard to please," I said, unsympathetically. "So many friends, so few problems, and yet you're still not content."

"Nelly, can you keep a secret?" she asked, kneeling beside me, lifting her lovely eyes to my face with a look that could melt anyone's bad temper.

"Is it worth keeping?" I asked, a little less sulkily.

"Yes. Today, Edgar Linton asked me to marry him and I've given him an answer. Before I tell you what it was, tell me what I should have said."

"Oh, Miss Catherine, how should I know?" I replied impatiently.

She jumped to her feet angrily. "Well, I accepted him! Tell me if I was wrong!"

"Do you love Mr Linton?" I asked.

"Who could help it? Of course I do," she answered.

"Why do you love him, Miss Catherine?" It was a tricky question but, at the age of twenty-two, she ought to have answered it with ease.

"Well, because he's handsome and pleasant to be with."

"Bad!" I remarked.

"And because he's young and cheerful."

"Still bad."

"And he's going to be rich, and I'd like to be the greatest woman of the neighbourhood."

"Worst of all. He won't always be handsome or young, and he might not always be rich."

"Well, I don't need your permission!"

"That's fine," I told her. "But tell me then – what are you unhappy about? You love Edgar; he loves you. What's the problem?"

"*Here*! and *here*!" cried Catherine, striking one hand on her forehead and the other on her chest. "In my soul and in my heart, I'm convinced I'm wrong!"

"That's very strange!" I said, **bewildered**.

She sat down beside me, her expression growing sadder and more serious, nervously **twisting** her fingers together in her lap.

"I had a dream, Nelly. I was in heaven and I was miserable."

"Because you don't belong there," I said. "All sinners would be miserable in heaven."

She laughed. "Heaven didn't feel like home and the angels were so angry that they **flung** me out into the middle of the moor, right on top of Wuthering Heights. And I woke up sobbing for joy. The point is, I have no more right to marry Edgar Linton than I have to be in heaven. And if my nasty brother hadn't treated Heathcliff so badly, I would never even have thought of being Edgar's wife. But it would **degrade** me to marry Heathcliff now so he'll never know how much I love him. And it's not because he's handsome, Nelly, but because he's more myself than I am. Whatever our souls are made of, his and mine are the same, and Edgar's is as different as frost from fire."

Before she'd finished speaking, I became aware of Heathcliff's presence. I turned my head just in time to see him get up and silently leave the room. He'd listened till he heard Catherine say it would degrade her to marry him.

Catherine didn't know he'd been listening.

"When you become Mrs Linton, it will make Heathcliff the unluckiest creature ever," I told her. "He'll lose his friend, his love, everything! Have you thought about that at all?"

"He won't lose anything!" she cried. "Every Linton on earth could melt into nothing before I would abandon Heathcliff. I'd never become Mrs Linton if it meant losing him. My love for Edgar is like the leaves in the woods: time will change it, as winter changes the trees. My love for Heathcliff is like the eternal rocks beneath: not beautiful to look at but necessary. Nelly, I *am* Heathcliff! He's always, always in my mind. He's part of me. So don't speak of our separation again."

She hid her face in the folds of my dress but I pulled it away angrily. "You don't understand marriage at all!" I said.

At that moment, Joseph came in. I whispered to Catherine that Heathcliff had heard part of her speech. She was absolutely distraught and ran out to look for him.

"Running after boys, as usual, is she?" muttered Joseph.

Catherine searched for Heathcliff for hours but she couldn't find him. Around midnight, there was a violent storm over Wuthering Heights, yet even then Catherine stubbornly refused to stop searching, getting thoroughly wet. The lightning split a great tree in half in the garden, sending a huge branch crashing onto the roof of the house and damaging it.

Catherine had finally given up her search and lain down on the sofa, but she refused to change out of her wet clothes. And when I came down the next morning, she was still there.

When she woke up and remembered Heathcliff had vanished, she burst into tears of grief. She cried and cried and would not calm down. I thought she'd gone mad. And soon I had to call the doctor, who told us she was dangerously ill. She had a fever.

I can't say I was a gentle nurse, although Joseph and the master were no better, and the headstrong Catherine wasn't an easy patient. But gradually, she got better.

Old Mrs Linton paid us several visits, ordering us to do this and that to help her future daughter-in-law. She regretted her kindness, though: she and her husband caught Catherine's illness and died within a few days of each other.

Heathcliff didn't return.

Edgar Linton doted on Catherine and believed himself the happiest man alive on the day he led Catherine to church, three years after his father's death.

As for me, I was forced to leave Wuthering Heights and my dear little Hareton, who was nearly five, and accompany my mistress to her new home at Thrushcross Grange.

* * * * *

At this point in her tale, the housekeeper glanced at the clock. Seeing it was half-past one, she wished me good night and went to bed.

Chapter 7

Four weeks of sickness! What a wonderful way to begin a life of solitude! Oh, these bleak winds, bitter northern skies and lazy country doctors!

I'm still too weak to read so why not call Mrs Dean up to finish her story? I remember her hero had run off and never been heard of for three years, and the heroine was married.

"Take your knitting out of your pocket," I suggested when she came up to my room, "and continue the story of Mr Heathcliff. Did he complete his education and come back a sophisticated gentleman or did he make his fortune robbing travellers on the road?"

"Perhaps, Mr Lockwood, but I have no idea. I told you before, I don't know how he made his money. But I'll carry on with the story in my own way, if you don't mind."

"Please do, Mrs Dean."

* * * * *

Miss Catherine **settled in** well at Thrushcross Grange, much better than I'd expected. She seemed almost too fond of Edgar and she was very kind to his sister, Isabella.

Edgar was careful never to upset his wife – her illness had frightened him and she was never as lively as she had been before. He told me off many times for speaking to her harshly, saying the stab of a knife couldn't hurt him more than seeing Catherine annoyed.

He was a kind master so I did as he asked and so did the other servants. For six months, all was peaceful and the married couple were, I believe, genuinely happy.

It didn't last.

One mild evening in September, I was returning from the garden with a heavy basket of apples. It was **dusk** and there were shadows everywhere. Suddenly, a deep voice called from behind me, "Nelly, is that you?"

I froze in fear. Turning, I saw a tall man with dark hair.

At first, I hardly dared believe it. Was it really him? Or was it a ghost? I **gasped**, raising my hands in amazement.

"Heathcliff?"

"Yes," he replied. Then, glancing towards the house, he asked, "Is she here?"

"Yes, she and Mr Linton are in the sitting room."

I took him inside, worried that the excitement of seeing him might be too much for my mistress.

Catherine jumped up from the sofa. "Oh, Heathcliff! You've come back!"

She ran to him, grabbing both his hands and leading him to Edgar. Taking her husband's **reluctant** fingers, she pushed them together with Heathcliff's.

By the light of the fire, I could clearly see how much Heathcliff had altered. I could hardly believe it. He'd grown tall and athletic, standing very upright, as if he'd been in the army. His face was intelligent without any sign of his former degradation. But his eyes were still full of black fire.

My master was as surprised as I was.

They all sat down, Catherine's eyes fixed on her old friend, as if she was afraid he'd vanish if she looked away. He was reserved at first but it soon became obvious that he took great pleasure in looking at her.

They were too absorbed in each other to notice Edgar growing pale. He became even more annoyed when Catherine jumped up and grabbed Heathcliff's hand, saying, "This will seem like a dream tomorrow! But it was cruel of you to disappear for three years without a thought for me!"

"I thought of you more than you did of me," he replied bitterly. "Since I last heard your voice, my life has been one long struggle, but I struggled only for you."

"Catherine, it's late," interrupted Edgar. "I'm sure Mr Heathcliff will want to leave soon."

I walked outside with Heathcliff and he informed me that

he was staying at Wuthering Heights, with Hindley. I was shocked. They hated each other!

"I went to see him," Heathcliff explained. "He was playing cards with some friends and invited me to join in the game. He lost and now owes me money but he didn't mind that. He said I must stay with him so we could play more."

I knew that it wasn't wise of Hindley to trust Heathcliff but he didn't realise his old enemy still wanted revenge. I suppose he was just pleased to get the money that Heathcliff would pay him for staying there.

That night, I heard Catherine and her husband arguing. He was jealous, of course, but she insisted he and Heathcliff must try to be friends for her sake. Edgar gave in and Heathcliff started visiting regularly.

However, soon there was a new source of trouble: Isabella Linton, at the time a charming lady of eighteen, was falling for the guest.

Her brother was **appalled** and not just because it would be a disgrace for his sister to marry a man of unknown family. If Isabella became Heathcliff's wife, and Edgar didn't have a male **heir**, his property would pass to Heathcliff! That thought was unbearable.

Catherine wasn't pleased when she found out either. "If

you think Heathcliff is hiding kindness and affection under his fierce appearance, you're an idiot!" she shouted. "He'd smash you like a bird's egg if he had the chance, Isabella! He could never love a Linton but he'd certainly marry you for your fortune."

"You're just jealous!" Isabella shouted back.

"Don't believe me, then!" answered Catherine. "But you'll regret it!"

Meanwhile, I began to hear rumours that Hindley was spending his nights drinking and **gambling** with Heathcliff and others. He was sinking into debt and had been borrowing money against his property.

Heathcliff's stay at Wuthering Heights made me feel anxious. I felt as though God had left a sheep wandering the moors alone and an evil beast was watching it, waiting for the right moment to jump on it and destroy it.

I wanted to see the situation at the house for myself so I walked there the following day. Looking through the gate, I spotted Hareton, *my* Hareton, not greatly altered since I'd left him ten months earlier.

"Hareton, it's Nelly!" I called out happily.

He stepped back and picked up a stone, clearly not recognising me. He swore and threw the stone at me. It hit my hat.

"Who taught you those words?" I asked sadly.

"Heathcliff."

"And does the priest still come to teach you to read and write?"

"No," he replied gruffly. "Heathcliff said he'd punch the priest in the face if he came near the house."

I returned home. I found Heathcliff in the kitchen with Catherine, arguing about his interest in Isabella.

"If you like her, marry her," Catherine said. "But I'm certain you don't."

"I'll take my revenge and you won't stop me! You've treated me terribly so why should I listen to you?" Heathcliff said.

At that moment, Edgar Linton walked in. "What are you doing here?" he asked. "Leave now and never come back. Your presence is like poison in my household."

"Are you going to hit me," Heathcliff **sneered**, "or are you too much of a coward?"

Edgar moved forward and, although pale and trembling, he struck his enemy hard in the throat. As Heathcliff gasped for breath, he left the room.

Once Heathcliff had recovered, he wanted to go after Edgar but I persuaded him not to. Instead, he returned to Wuthering Heights.

Catherine collapsed onto the sofa in the living room, distraught.

"Why is Edgar so unreasonable?" she complained. "I could have convinced Heathcliff not to marry Isabella but now it's hopeless. Well, if I can't keep Heathcliff as my friend, and if Edgar's going to be mean and jealous, I'll break both their hearts by breaking my own. Edgar will find out how passionate my nature really is!"

Edgar came in to find her hitting her head against the sofa, then she stretched out her body, going white as a sheet and looking like death.

Her husband was terrified. "She has blood on her lips!" he cried, trembling.

"Never mind," I answered coldly. "She's making herself look crazy and ill for your attention and sympathy."

She heard me and jumped up, her hair flying over her shoulders and her eyes flashing. I thought she was going to break my bones in anger but, instead, she rushed from the room.

She locked herself in her bedroom, refusing to come out or eat anything for two days.

During that time, Edgar stayed in his study, never once asking how his wife was. He spoke to Isabella, warning her that, if she went ahead with her plan to marry that **worthless** beast, he'd no longer consider her his sister.

Chapter 8

On the third day, Catherine unlocked her door and asked for some more water and some food, claiming she was dying.

I didn't believe her so I didn't tell the master. I just took her some tea and toast. She ate and drank eagerly, then fell back against the pillow, twisting her hands together and complaining bitterly. "He doesn't love me. I don't want to make him happy by dying. What's the pathetic man doing? Is he dead?"

"He's fine," I answered without emotion. "He's busy in his study with his books."

"With his books!" she cried. "While I'm dying?"

Suddenly, she fixed her eyes on something at the other end of the room. "Nelly, look at the black cupboard. There's a face in it!"

I turned to look but all I saw was a mirror. I told her she was wrong but she didn't believe me. "Don't you see the face?"

I got up and covered the mirror with a blanket.

"It's behind there still!" she said anxiously. "And it's moving. Who is it? Oh, Nelly, the room's haunted! I'm afraid of being alone!"

I took her hand and tried to **reassure** her. "It's *you*, Catherine!"

"Oh," she said quietly. "My mind must be confused because I'm so weak."

She suddenly sat up. "Open the window, Nelly! I want to feel the wind on my face. It comes across the moor, from my old home. I miss it so much. Let me feel the wind!"

It was the middle of winter and the wind that night was fierce. I told her it wasn't a good idea but she grew so upset that I finally gave in. As I opened the window, the cold wind blew savagely into the room.

"They can bury me four metres deep," she cried out into the darkness, "but I won't rest until you're with me, Heathcliff! I wish I were a child again, with you, half savage and free. I don't belong here. I'm among strangers, an outcast."

Her face was wet with tears. I tried to pull her away from the window but she was surprisingly strong.

The next moment, Edgar entered the room, drawn by the sound of our voices.

"Oh, sir," I said desperately, "help me! My poor mistress is ill but she won't go to bed, and it's nearly midnight."

"Catherine, ill?" he said, rushing forwards. "Shut the

window, Nelly."

He looked at Catherine's pale, exhausted face, his eyes filled with worry. "Why didn't you tell me?" he accused me, taking his wife in his arms.

She didn't recognise him at first but then, with sudden anger, she said, "Ah, Edgar Linton, you've come. Listen, I don't want to be buried with the Lintons inside the church, do you hear me? I want to be buried in the open air."

Edgar's voice trembled. "Don't you love me anymore, Catherine? Do you love that beast, Heath—"

"Shh!" Catherine interrupted. "If you mention his name, I'll jump out the window. I don't want you, Edgar. Return to your books."

The doctor was called. He reported that Catherine would only recover if we kept her calm and avoided upsetting her.

The next morning, a servant came to me, looking panicked. Isabella wasn't in her room. "The boy that delivers the milk saw her with Mr Heathcliff two miles from Gimmerton village", she said. "They've run away together."

I hesitated to tell my master, knowing how much he already had to bear. But I needn't have worried. When I went to let him know, he was sitting by Catherine's bed and merely answered calmly, "It was her choice to go. She's no longer my sister and I don't want to hear another word about her."

Chapter 9

For two months, the disgraced couple remained absent. Meanwhile, Catherine's health gradually improved. No mother would have tended an only child more devotedly than Edgar tended her.

But her mind never recovered.

The first time she left her bedroom was at the beginning of March. We helped her down to the living room and settled her in an armchair by the window, where the sunlight warmed her pale face.

Her husband brought her some golden flowers. She was delighted with them. "These are the earliest flowers at Wuthering Heights!" she cried. "Has the snow melted, Edgar?"

"Yes, my darling," he said gently. "I can only see two white spots on the whole moor. The sky is blue and the birds are singing. Catherine, this time last spring, I was **longing** to have you under this roof. Now, I wish you were a mile or two up those hills. The wind blows so sweetly, I feel that it would cure you."

"I'll never be there except once more," said the patient,

"and when I am, you'll leave me, and I'll remain there forever. Next spring, you'll long to have me under this roof again, and you'll look back and think you were happy today."

Edgar tried to cheer her up but she only gazed at the flowers, tears collecting on her eyelashes and running down her cheeks.

Being in the living room was a welcome change and she was reluctant to return upstairs. In any case, she was too weak to keep going up and down the stairs, so we arranged the sofa as her bed.

Ah, I thought myself, perhaps she'll recover, so well cared for as she is. And I prayed for that, for my master's sake because soon an heir would be born. Catherine was pregnant.

Several weeks after her departure, Isabella sent her brother a brief note, announcing her marriage to Heathcliff. It was cold and formal but, at the bottom, she'd added an apology in pencil.

Edgar didn't reply to it.

A fortnight later, I got a long letter from her. It was a strange letter for a bride to write so soon after her honeymoon. I kept it so I'll read it to you.

* * * * *

Dear Nelly,

I arrived at Wuthering Heights last night. I must write to someone and, since my brother clearly doesn't want to hear from me, you're my only option.

Inform Edgar that my heart returned to Thrushcross Grange almost as soon as I left it, and it's there now, full of warm feelings for him and Catherine. *I can't follow it though.* As for the reason, they may draw whatever conclusions they wish.

Nelly, I have two questions for you.

First, how did you manage to remain kind and good-hearted while living here?

Second – and this is of great interest to me – is Heathcliff a man? If so, is he mad? And if not, is he a devil? I won't tell you my reasons for asking but please explain, if you can, what I have married.

When we first arrived at the house, Heathcliff had work to do so I went inside alone. In the kitchen, I found a rough, slovenly child with eyes that reminded me of Catherine's. Realising he must be Edgar's nephew, I stepped forward, held out my hand, and said, "Let's be friends, Hareton."

He swore at me and warned that, if I didn't leave him alone, Throttler, his dog, would attack me. At that moment, the animal growled **menacingly** so I quickly left the room.

Joseph was no less rude and sat muttering to himself.

I felt ridiculous in my fine silk dress in that dirty, messy place. You wouldn't recognise it, Nelly.

In the courtyard, I came across a tall, **gaunt** man, also very slovenly and also with eyes like Catherine's, though without their beauty. It was Hindley.

"Who are you?" he demanded gruffly.

"My maiden name was Isabella Linton," I answered. "You've seen me before. I've just got married to Mr Heathcliff, and he's brought me here."

He growled that he was glad "the devil from hell" had kept his promise to return. Then, pulling a gun from his pocket, he added menacingly, "I go upstairs with this every night and try to open Heathcliff's door. If he ever forgets to lock it, he's a dead man."

I took it from his hand and gazed at it, thinking how powerful I would be if I could keep it. Hindley grabbed it back, his face dark with jealousy.

"Why don't you tell Heathcliff to leave?" I asked.

"No!" he shouted. "I won't lose everything before I've had the chance to win it back. I'll take back what's mine, and I'll have his blood too. Hell can have his soul!"

I went back inside and sat by the fire, in miserable solitude, remembering that four miles away was my delightful home, containing the only people I loved on earth. But those four miles might as well be the Atlantic Ocean. And there's nobody here to protect me from Heathcliff.

A while later, my *darling* husband came into the house and immediately started threatening me. He told me about Catherine's illness (poor Catherine!) and accused my brother of causing it. Then, with a terrible look in his eyes, he told me that, until he could take his revenge on Edgar, he'd make *me* suffer instead. He wants to kill him and drink his blood, but he says he won't touch a hair on his head – yet – because Catherine wouldn't want that.

"I was a fool to think that she valued Edgar Linton more than me," he continued. "He couldn't love her as much in eighty years as I could in a single day."

I answered proudly that my brother and Catherine were very fond of each other and that he should stop insulting him.

"Edgar's clearly *very* fond of you, too," he sneered. "He hasn't hesitated to abandon you."

I hate Heathcliff. And he hates me. I was an idiot to think he was some kind of romantic hero.

Don't tell my brother any of this.

Isabella

Chapter 10

Another week is over and I'm seven days nearer health, and spring! Mrs Dean has now told me all of my neighbour's story and I'll continue in her own words. I don't think I could improve her style.

* * * * *

One warm and pleasant evening (the housekeeper said), the others went to church but Catherine stayed at home. She sat in a loose white dress by an open window. She'd altered a lot since her illness. She was calm now and the flash of her eyes had been replaced by a melancholy softness. She no longer looked *at* objects; she gazed *through* them, into another world, it seemed.

She was no longer as gaunt as during her illness, but her face was so pale that I knew she was doomed to die.

As the church bells rang in the distance, I saw someone approaching the house. It was Heathcliff and of course he couldn't resist the open window. He climbed in, **strode** towards Catherine and grasped her in his arms.

I was too surprised to act.

For a full five minutes, he held her tightly and they kept kissing and kissing. When he finally leant back and looked at her face, he was shocked. He clearly felt, as I did, that she was doomed.

"Oh, Cathy! How can I bear it?" was the first thing he said, staring at her, his eyes burning.

Catherine looked back at him. "You and Edgar have broken my heart, Heathcliff! And you both expect me to feel sorry for you, but why should I? You've killed me without suffering at all for it, it seems. You look so fit and healthy! How many years do you intend to live after I'm gone?"

Heathcliff had knelt down to hug her. He tried to get up but she seized his hair, keeping him down.

"I wish I could hold you until we were both dead!" she continued bitterly. "I wouldn't care if you suffered. Why shouldn't you suffer? *I* do! Will you forget me? Will you be happy when I'm in the earth?"

To a calm spectator, they made a strange and frightening picture. Catherine had been right to claim that heaven would be no home for her.

Heathcliff pulled his head free but Catherine kept in her closed fist a **lock** of the hair she'd been grasping.

"You know you're lying – I haven't killed you," said Heathcliff. "And Catherine, you know I'd forget my own existence before I could ever forget you! Isn't it enough for your horrible selfishness that while you're at peace, I'll be in hell?"

"I won't be at peace," complained Catherine, her heart beating so violently that she could hear it.

She waited until she felt calmer again, then said more gently, "I only want for us always to be together. If you feel distraught after I'm dead, just remember that I'm just as distraught underground, and forgive me! Come here and kneel down again! You never harmed me in your life."

He refused to go back to her and turned instead to the fireplace.

"Heathcliff, stop sulking," she continued. "Come here."

When he didn't, she got up, **supporting** herself on the arm of the chair. He turned to her, his eyes flashing fiercely. They stayed apart for a moment, then Catherine moved forwards and he caught her. They held each other so tightly that I was worried my mistress would never be released alive!

I moved towards them but he growled at me like a mad dog and clung to her even more tightly, with greedy jealousy. In that moment, I didn't feel he was a creature of my own species.

His cheek pressed against hers, he said, "Why did you

betray your own heart, Cathy? You deserve this. You've killed yourself. You loved me – then what *right* did you have to marry Edgar? Answer me! Misery, degradation, death, even the devil himself, *nothing* could have separated us, but *you* did it. I deserve pity for being strong. What kind of life will I have when you ... Oh, God! Would *you* like to live with your soul in the grave?"

"If I made a mistake, I'm dying for it," sobbed Catherine. "That's enough! You left me too but I forgive you. Forgive *me*!"

"I do," he cried. "Kiss me again but don't let me see your eyes. I love *my* murderer – but how can I love yours?"

Their faces were hidden against each other and washed by each other's tears.

Looking out, I saw my master coming in through the gate. I told Heathcliff to leave immediately and he did, although Catherine cried out for him to remain.

"I'll stay near the house," he promised.

As he walked out, her head fell back against the chair. She had fainted.

At about twelve o'clock that night, the Catherine you saw at Wuthering Heights was born. She was a **puny** baby, who came two months early.

Two hours later, her mother died.

It's too painful to **dwell on** Edgar's grief but the depth of his sadness became clear as time passed.

On top of that, Edgar was left without an heir. The child was a daughter, who could never inherit the estate.

In death, Catherine looked at peace, and no angel in heaven could be more beautiful than she appeared.

Edgar stayed by her side but finally, exhausted, he left the room to sleep for a couple of hours. I opened one of the windows, knowing that Heathcliff was waiting in the garden and would want to say goodbye.

I left the room and, when I returned, I could tell immediately that he'd been there. On the floor lay a lock of light hair, which I knew had been taken from the **locket** around Catherine's neck. Heathcliff had opened it, removed its contents and replaced them with a lock of his own black hair. Picking up Edgar's hair, I twisted it together with Heathcliff's and placed them both into the locket.

To the surprise of our neighbours, Catherine was buried not in the church with the Lintons, nor with her own relatives. Instead, she was buried on a green slope in a corner of the churchyard, where the wall is so low that there's a view of the moors. Her husband lies in the same spot now.

Chapter 11

The evening after the funeral, the weather changed. My master stayed in his room and I sat with a crying baby in my arms, watching the snow fall outside.

Suddenly, the door burst open and someone entered, out of breath and laughing!

"I've run the whole way from Wuthering Heights!" said a familiar voice. "Don't worry, Nelly. I'll explain everything."

It was Isabella, covered in snow, her wet clothes clinging to her. A deep cut below one ear sent blood running down her neck.

After she changed into dry clothes, we sat down by the fire together.

"My husband's a beast!" she cried, pulling off her wedding ring and throwing it into the fire. "And Edgar hasn't been kind to me either," she added angrily. "I don't want to see him."

"Calm down and drink your tea," I told her, handing the baby to another servant.

She didn't listen. "Whenever Heathcliff looks at me, I

can tell he hates me because I remind him of Edgar. He won't try and find me if I run away."

"You want to run away?" I asked, concerned.

"I have to! It's not safe for me at Wuthering Heights. That man isn't human!"

"Don't say that," I replied. "Of course he's human. There are worse men." Then I asked, "Why have you come here?"

"Last night, I was sitting in the living room, my mind going back again and again to that new grave in the churchyard. Hindley, sitting opposite me and drunk as usual, suddenly said, 'I'm going to murder Heathcliff tonight. He's destroyed my life so he must die!' His eyes were full of rage.

"I argued with him but he replied, 'His death will make you a free woman, and Hareton will finally get justice!'

"I understood what he meant, of course. With all his gambling, Hindley owed Heathcliff huge amounts of money. If Heathcliff died, Hareton would be out of his control and would eventually inherit the estate.

"Heathcliff had been out on the moors but the storm brought him home. As he came into the room, I shouted to him that Hindley had a gun. Heathcliff ran towards him and tried to take it from his grasp.

"As they struggled, the gun fired by accident. Hindley collapsed, blood pouring from the wound. Heathcliff kicked him, then grabbed his head and smashed it against the floor several times, holding me back with one hand.

"Then, seeming to regret his violence a little, he took off Hindley's coat and wrapped it tightly around the wound.

"This morning, I found Hindley on the sofa, looking very ill.

"When Heathcliff came downstairs, I felt so angry that I couldn't resist shouting, 'Are you determined to murder all the Earnshaws? Everyone knows Catherine would still be alive if it wasn't for you!'

"'Get out of my sight!' Heathcliff shouted back, his eyes full of tears. Then he threw a dinner knife at me. It hit me below the ear, as you see.

"I ran out, knocking over Hareton, who'd been busy hanging four puppies from the back of a chair.

"I can't ever go back there."

Although I begged her to stay, she wasn't prepared to. She kissed Edgar's and Catherine's portraits, and my cheek, then left.

She made London her new home and there, she had a son, who she named Linton. She wrote to Edgar that he was a weak, puny baby.

Heathcliff found out about the child (I don't know how) but he didn't bother Isabella about him. However, one day he said to me menacingly, "When I want it, I'll have it."

The day after Isabella's unexpected visit, I informed Edgar that his sister had run away. Grief has changed him so deeply that he didn't react much.

He rarely even left the house anymore, except to visit his wife's grave. But he was too good to be thoroughly unhappy for long and, over the years, his mood gradually improved. He was a sharp contrast to Hindley, who'd also lost a wife he was devoted to but reacted much worse. Hindley seemed strong but was actually weak.

Hindley's end came only six months after his sister's. We at Thrushcross Grange never got a precise account of what happened. I only know from the doctor that he died drunk at the age of only twenty-seven. That's my age.

He'd borrowed huge amounts of money from Heathcliff, using Wuthering Heights to pay off his debts. This meant that, when he died, Heathcliff took control of the house and Hindley's son was left with nothing. This is part of his revenge. Unless Heathcliff decides to help him, Hareton lives in his own house as a servant, unaware of the truth.

(I asked Mrs Dean whether Heathcliff had killed Hindley but she admitted that nobody knew.)

I convinced my master to ask Heathcliff if his nephew Hareton could come and live with us at Thrushcross Grange, but Heathcliff's answer soon stopped our attempts. "If you take Hareton, I'll replace him with my own son from London."

For a while, Edgar didn't even notice his daughter but his coldness melted as fast as the snow in April. She was named Catherine but he never called her that – she was always Cathy.

Chapter 12

The twelve years following that awful period, continued Mrs Dean, were the happiest of my life. Little Cathy brought sunshine into a melancholy house and she was a real beauty, with the Earnshaws' lovely dark eyes and the Lintons' fair skin, small features and curly blonde hair.

She had a strong personality but she was also sensitive. She formed strong attachments to people, just like her mother, and she was affectionate like her. But she was gentler than Catherine had been and her anger was never furious.

She wasn't perfect, though. She could be **sassy** and her father spoilt her, never once speaking a harsh word to her.

Until the age of thirteen, she hadn't ever left her father's estate by herself. Wuthering Heights and Heathcliff did not exist for her. She would sometimes ask what was beyond the hills and I would just reply, "Nothing interesting, miss."

One day, my master received a letter from his sister to say that she was dying. She begged him to come and get her son – she wanted him to live with us. Usually reluctant to leave the house, Edgar didn't hesitate to rush to London immediately.

He was away three weeks and Cathy became impatient. It was a beautiful summer and she got in the habit of going for long rides without me. One day, she asked permission to stay out for a few hours. I agreed, trusting her because I thought she'd be too scared to leave the estate on her own.

I was wrong.

When she didn't come home for dinner, I panicked and went to look for her, but saw no sign. At last, a farm worker told me he'd seen her jump over the fence of the estate on her horse, earlier in the day. He showed me the direction she'd gone, which was towards the part of the moor by Wuthering Heights.

You can guess how I felt hearing this news. I walked mile after mile, eventually arriving at Heathcliff's house. A servant told me that the owner wasn't at home, and I was relieved to hear it.

I found Cathy inside. She must have found the place by chance. She looked perfectly at home, laughing and chatting to Hareton, now a big, strong young man of eighteen. He was good-looking but dressed like a farm worker. He stared at her with great curiosity and amazement.

"Do you know whose house this is?" I asked her angrily, my hands on my hips.

"It's your father's, isn't it?" said she, turning to Hareton.

"No," he replied, looking down and blushing shyly.

"Whose then – your master's?" she asked.

He swore at her, turning as black as a thundercloud. I told her we should leave.

"Get my horse," she ordered the young man.

"Damn you!" he growled. "I'm not a servant!"

"Nelly, how dare he speak to me like that?" she cried in shock.

"Talk to him nicely, miss," I whispered. "Hareton's your cousin."

"My cousin?" she sneered. "That's not right. Father's gone to fetch my cousin from London."

"People can have more than one cousin," I said. She started to cry, not wanting to believe it.

Hareton must have felt guilty for being so harsh with her because he brought her horse to her after all. On the way home, I made her promise not to tell her father about her adventure, explaining that he objected to the whole household at Wuthering Heights. I warned her that, if he found out she'd been there, he might sack me.

Cathy couldn't bear that prospect so she promised to keep the visit secret for my sake. She was a sweet girl.

The day of my master's return finally arrived. Cathy was

wild with joy about meeting her "real" cousin, Linton. "He's only six months younger than me," she said excitedly. "It'll be such fun playing with him."

When she saw her father, she ran to him eagerly and hugged him. Then she turned to look at her cousin. He was pale and delicate, and wrapped in a fur coat, as if it were winter. He looked like Edgar's younger brother, they were so alike. But, unlike my master, he looked impatient and **whiny**.

Cathy wanted to run around and play with him straight away but her father said gently, "Linton isn't as strong or lively as you, and he's just lost his mother. Let's give him time to settle in, alright?"

Later that evening, while Cathy was stroking her cousin's curly hair and kissing his cheek, Joseph arrived from Wuthering Heights, asking to speak to my master.

"What do you want?" I asked.

"Mr Heathcliff has sent me for his son."

Hearing this, Edgar's face filled with sadness. His sister had asked him to look after her boy and he didn't want to give him up to his father. He searched in his heart for a solution but couldn't find one.

"Tell Mr Heathcliff," he said calmly, "that his son will come to Wuthering Heights tomorrow. He's too tired after his long journey to come tonight."

"The master insisted I get his son straight away," said Joseph.

"No!" answered Edgar angrily.

So Joseph went back to Wuthering Heights without the boy.

Chapter 13

My master told me to take the boy to Wuthering Heights early the next morning. "And don't tell my daughter where he's gone. They must never interact again so it's important she doesn't find out how nearby he'll be. It would make her want to visit Wuthering Heights."

Linton was reluctant to be woken at five o'clock. I tried to encourage him by explaining that he was going to meet his father, Mr Heathcliff.

"My father?" he cried in confusion. "Mother never told me I had a father. I'd rather stay with Uncle."

"You should be glad to finally meet him," I said, not really believing my own words. "Try to love him, as you did your mother, and then he'll love you."

He started whining that he didn't want to go and, in the end, I had to ask for my master's help to get him out of bed. Finally, we set off.

We arrived at Wuthering Heights and went inside.

"Morning, Nelly!" said Heathcliff when he saw me. "I thought I'd have to come and fetch my property myself. You've brought it, have you? Let me see it."

Getting up from his chair, he strode over to us. He stared at his son, then burst out laughing.

"God, what a beauty!" he cried. "That's worse than I expected and the devil knows I wasn't hopeful."

Linton clung to me, hiding his face in my dress and sobbing.

Heathcliff pulled him roughly towards him. "Stop that nonsense! I won't hurt you. You're your mother's child, entirely! Where's my share in you, you puny thing?" Then he turned to me. "Thanks for bringing him, Nelly. You can go now."

"Well," I replied, "I hope you'll be kind to the boy, Mr Heathcliff, or he won't survive – he's so delicate. And he's your only blood relative in the whole world, remember."

"Oh, I'll be *very* kind to him, don't worry," he said, laughing. "Joseph, bring the boy some breakfast."

Turning back to me, he said, "You're right, Nelly. I should take good care of him. After all, my son might inherit your place and I don't want him to die before I'm certain I'll inherit it after him. That's the only reason I'll tolerate this pathetic brat. Aside from that, I hate him – for who he is and for the memories he brings. But he's safe with me and I've even arranged for a tutor to come to the house. I only wish he was worthy of my pride. I'm bitterly disappointed in the whining coward."

Joseph brought in some breakfast and placed it in front of Linton, who took one look at it and cried sulkily, "I won't eat it! Take it away!"

I suggested boiled milk instead, then left quietly, having no more reason to stay. But Linton noticed my departure and, as I closed the door, I heard a desperate cry: "Don't leave me! I refuse to stay here!"

Someone locked the door from inside, and I rode home alone.

We had a difficult time with Cathy that day. She got up full of excitement, eager to spend time with her cousin, but she cried passionate tears when we revealed that he'd gone.

Even I felt a sense of grief that the boy hadn't been allowed to stay with us. I heard from the housekeeper at Wuthering Heights that Heathcliff could hardly bear to be in the same room as him and the boy himself had become even more whiny and unpleasant since he'd moved there. "He doesn't get on with Hareton either," she told me. "Hareton's not bad-natured, although he's rough, but they're always arguing, one swearing and the other crying. I think the master would take pleasure in seeing Hareton beat him, if Linton weren't his son."

Time passed in its former pleasant way until Miss Cathy reached sixteen. We never celebrated her birthday because it was also the anniversary of her mother's death. Her father always spent the day in his study and walked to the churchyard, at dusk, often staying there till midnight. So Cathy had to entertain herself.

The twentieth of March that year was a beautiful spring day and Cathy came to ask me to accompany her on a walk to the edge of the moor. I agreed and we set off.

I was enjoying myself, watching my darling running in the warm sunshine, her golden curls flying loose behind her, her eyes bright with pleasure. She was a happy creature, and an angel, in those days. It's a shame she couldn't be content.

"Let's go a little further, Nelly," she cried enthusiastically and I followed behind her. Suddenly, I realised we were only two miles from Wuthering Heights and I saw her talking to two people, some distance ahead.

One of them was Heathcliff.

As I reached them, Cathy was talking about her father. Heathcliff noticed me and, with a menacing smile, asked her, "And who is your father?"

"Mr Linton of Thrushcross Grange," she replied. Then she pointed at Hareton and asked, "Who's that? Is he your son? I think I've seen him before."

Hareton looked bigger and stronger than two years earlier but just as awkward and rough as ever.

Heathcliff informed her that Hareton was not his son but that he had a son at home. "You've seen *him* before, too."

Cathy insisted that she'd never met his son. Heathcliff then invited us to come and rest at the house. I whispered to Cathy that she must not, under any circumstances, accept the invitation but she ignored me.

Heathcliff seized my arm so I couldn't stop Cathy walking merrily into the house. "You know this isn't a good idea, Mr Heathcliff!" I cried.

"Oh, it's an excellent idea," he laughed. "I want those two to fall in love and get married. But don't worry, Nelly. I'm being generous to your master – you know his daughter won't inherit anything, but if she does as I wish, she'll immediately share Linton's inheritance."

"If Linton died," I answered, "and his life is quite uncertain, Catherine would be the heir."

"No, she wouldn't," he said. "There's no clause in the **will** to guarantee that: his property would go to me."

Heathcliff led me into the house. Linton, who was now nearly sixteen, had grown tall. His features were pretty and his eyes were brighter than I remembered.

"So, you see," Heathcliff announced happily to Cathy while pointing to his son, "you *have* met before!"

"Linton!" cried Cathy in great surprise. "It's you!"

The boy stepped forward and Cathy kissed him enthusiastically. Then they stepped back and looked at each other. Cathy sparkled with health and liveliness; Linton was elegant but lacked energy.

Cathy then turned her attention to Heathcliff. "So you're my uncle?" she asked him. "Why don't you ever visit us? Nelly, you're very naughty – why did you hide all this from me? I'll visit you often from now on, Mr Heathcliff. Can I?"

"Of course," said Heathcliff. "But I should tell you that your father has a prejudice against me. We had a massive argument before you were born and, if you mention coming here to him, he won't allow you to come again."

"You can visit now and then," Linton said to his cousin, "but not more than once or twice a week. Any more often would be too exhausting for me."

The father **glared** at his son, his eyes full of hate.

"Do you know, Nelly," Heathcliff said, turning to me, "twenty times a day, I wish Hareton were my son instead, despite all his degradation? But *she* (looking at Cathy) could never love him. I don't think that one (looking at Linton) will last till he's eighteen. Damn the pathetic idiot!"

"Mr Heathcliff, Hareton isn't my cousin, is he?" Cathy asked him.

"Yes, he is. He's your mother's nephew," Heathcliff answered. "Don't you like him? Isn't he handsome?"

The sassy girl looked at her cousin and then whispered something in Heathcliff's ear. He laughed. Hareton looked angry. He was very sensitive to insults, especially from Cathy, who he knew was superior to him.

"Go and show your cousin around," Heathcliff told Hareton. He obeyed and the two young people went outside together, barely talking.

Linton, sat by the fire wrapped in a blanket although it was a warm day, soon felt jealous and followed them.

The window was open and I heard their conversation. Cathy asked Hareton the meaning behind the writing above the front door. Hareton stared up, scratching his head in confusion.

"It's some stupid writing," he answered. "I can't read it."

"Can't read it?" Cathy repeated. "*I* can read it – it's English. But I want to know why it's there."

"He can't read!" Linton told his cousin. "He's an idiot! And have you noticed his awful Yorkshire accent?"

The two rude things burst into laughter.

"Linton, if you weren't more a girl than a boy," Hareton threatened, "I'd knock you over right now!" His face burnt with rage and embarrassment.

We stayed for a while longer, then walked home. We'd been gone many hours, but my master hadn't noticed.

Chapter 14

Cathy was too excited to keep the meeting a secret for long. "Father!" she cried the next morning. "Guess who we saw yesterday!" And she gave a full account of her adventure and its consequences.

While she was talking, my master kept glancing at me angrily. Then he listed all the reasons that Cathy should avoid interacting with the household at Wuthering Heights but, unfortunately, he didn't express himself **forcefully** enough.

"I knew that you couldn't stay friends with your cousin without coming into contact with Mr Heathcliff," he explained calmly. "He's an unkind man who takes pleasure in harming others."

"But Mr Heathcliff was very pleasant, Father," said Cathy, not at all convinced.

My master went on to explain that Heathcliff had treated her Aunt Isabella very badly and he explained how exactly Wuthering Heights had become his property. This shocked Cathy who, although passionate, had a sunny temperament and couldn't imagine anyone being angry enough to continue seeking revenge for so many years.

She kissed her father and sat down quietly to her lessons.

However, that evening, I found her crying. "Silly girl!" I said. "If you had any real problems, you wouldn't waste a tear on this. How would you feel if your father and I were dead? You should be grateful for the life you have."

"I'm not crying for myself, Nelly," she answered. "I'm crying for Linton. He expected to see me again tomorrow and he'll be so disappointed. He'll wait for me, and I won't come!"

"Nonsense!" I said. "Do you imagine he's thought as much of you as you have of him? Hasn't he got Hareton for a companion?"

"Can't I write him a note telling him why I can't come?" she asked, getting up and moving towards her desk.

"No, you can't!" I replied forcefully. "Then he'd write back and there'd be no end to it. Your father expects you not to see or contact him again. Get into bed at once."

She gave me a very sassy look, so sassy that I didn't kiss her good night at first, and I slammed the door as I left her room. But, regretting my harshness, I returned softly and what did I see? Miss Cathy at her desk with a piece of paper in front of her and a pencil in her hand!

She started when she noticed me. "Nobody will deliver

that for you, Cathy," I said **sternly**. I blew out her candle and left the room again.

The letter was finished and arrived at its destination, taken by a village boy who delivered our milk, although I didn't find this out until some time afterwards.

She kept going down to the kitchen very early and disappearing into corners with something in her hand, so I quickly became suspicious. It didn't take me long to find her huge collection of letters. They started off quite reserved. However, gradually, they expanded into enthusiastic love letters. They were mostly silly, as you would expect from such a young writer, but there were some sections that seemed to be influenced by a more experienced mind. Whether they satisfied Cathy I don't know, but they appeared complete nonsense to me.

I burnt the letters and, when Cathy discovered my betrayal, she became very angry. However, when I threatened to tell her father about them, she calmed down.

She was still upset though and started crying as if her heart would break. "I didn't want to fall in love with him but—"

"*Fall in love!*" I interrupted with a sneer. "I've never heard anything so ridiculous! If I told you I was madly in love with the clockmaker who comes once a year to repair our clocks, wouldn't you think I was crazy?"

"That's not the same thing at all!" Cathy cried. And she sulked for the rest of the day.

Summer came to an end and it was soon September. Edgar and his daughter often went for walks together and, on one occasion, they stayed out till dusk. The evening was damp and cold and this resulted in my master catching a cold, which unfortunately went onto his lungs. He had to stay inside nearly the whole winter.

The poor girl became considerably sadder and less lively after her father's illness. I tried to make up for the loss of his company, as much as possible, but I knew I was a poor substitute because I could only spare two or three hours a day from my duties.

One wet November afternoon, when the cold sky was hidden by clouds, Cathy insisted we went for our daily walk. She walked sadly, her head down: she never ran anymore.

"Look, Cathy!" I said, desperate to cheer her up. "Winter isn't here yet. There's a pretty little blue flower by the bank of the stream, the last one left. Why don't you climb down and pick it for your father?"

Cathy stared for a long time at the lonely flower trembling by the flowing water and at last replied, "No, I won't touch it. It looks melancholy, doesn't it, Nelly?"

"Yes," I agreed, "as sad and lonely as you. But let's not dwell on that. Your cheeks are so pale – take my hand and run with me to the bottom of that hill."

"No," she answered quietly.

We kept walking and I noticed she lifted her hand more than once to her face, which was turned away from me.

"Cathy, love, why are you crying?" I asked, putting my arm around her shoulder. "You mustn't cry because your father has a cold. Be glad it's nothing worse."

She finally let her tears flow, barely able to breathe from sobbing.

"But it *will* be something worse," she said. "And what will I do when you and Father leave me, and I'm all alone? I can't forget what you said, Nelly – how miserable my life will be, when you and Father are dead."

I tried to tell her that my master was young and I was strong and only forty-five. We weren't going to die any time soon! But my words didn't help. "I pray for Father every night, Nelly," she said. "But I don't suppose it will do any good."

On our way back, we walked along a road. To our surprise, we saw Heathcliff coming the other way.

He greeted us but Cathy replied sulkily, "I won't speak

to you, Mr Heathcliff. My father says you're an unkind man, and you hate both him and me. And Nelly says the same."

"Well, I don't hate my son," Heathcliff answered, "so let me talk to you about him. He's dying for you. You used to write to him but you stopped suddenly. He's in love with you and has never recovered from the disappointment. He's very unwell but a kind word from you would be his best medicine."

"How can you lie like that to the poor child?" I shouted furiously. "Come on, Cathy, we're leaving."

We started walking away but I could tell that Cathy's heart now felt a double sadness, for her father and for Linton. Her features were so sad that they didn't seem hers.

Chapter 15

Cathy was just as miserable the next day so I agreed to accompany the headstrong girl to Wuthering Heights. "I'll never be at ease until I see him again," she said.

The weather was misty and, by the time we arrived, my feet were thoroughly wet. We entered the farmhouse through the kitchen, where Joseph was sitting by the fire, clearly enjoying what he considered his idea of heaven. A glass of beer and a pile of biscuits sat on the table beside him.

"Is your master home?" I asked.

He remained silent for so long that I thought he'd gone deaf so I repeated my question more loudly.

"No!" he growled. "And you can leave me alone!"

"Joseph!" came an impatient voice from the next room. "Why are you ignoring me? Come here at once!"

Joseph didn't move.

We stepped into the room. "I hope you suffer a long, slow death!" said Linton, incorrectly assuming the grumpy servant had finally come in.

Then, realising who it was, his voice became softer. "Oh,

it's you, Cathy," he said, raising his head from the armchair. "No, don't kiss me – I can't breathe! Father said you'd come. Will you shut the door, please? You left it open, like Joseph did, and it's freezing in here! Why didn't you come sooner?"

"I wanted to," Cathy assured him, kneeling beside him and stroking his hair.

"You should have come, instead of writing. It was exhausting writing those long letters. Please come more often. I wouldn't be bad-tempered with you because you always do what I ask you, don't you? Father says if you were my wife, we'd be always together and you'd love me more than anyone."

"Not necessarily," Cathy replied. "People sometimes hate their husbands or wives. After all, your father hated your mother. That's why she left him."

I tried to stop her revealing this to Linton but she wouldn't stop talking.

"Well, I'll tell *you* something!" replied Linton, suddenly furious. "Your mother hated your father, and she loved mine."

"You little liar! I hate you now!" cried Cathy, her face burning with anger.

"She did! She did!" sang Linton.

In a rage, Cathy kicked his chair so hard that he fell against one arm. He was immediately seized by a **suffocating** cough, which lasted so long that it frightened even me.

As for his cousin, she burst into tears. "I'm sorry, Linton! I'm sorry!"

"Hareton never touches me," he complained weakly. "He's never hit me in his life. But you come here and you straight away try and kill me."

"I didn't hit you!" Cathy insisted.

They sat in silence for a while. But I noticed that, every time Cathy glanced in his direction, Linton coughed again, on purpose to upset her.

"We're going," I said at last, getting up.

As we turned to leave, Linton collapsed onto the floor, screaming.

"I'll lift him onto the sofa," I said impatiently, "and then we really are going."

Cathy hurried to put a cushion under his head.

"It's not high enough," Linton whined.

She brought another one.

"That's *too* high!" complained the annoying child.

"Oh, what do you want me to do then?" Cathy sighed.

He wrapped himself around her, as she knelt by his side,

supporting his head on her shoulder.

"No, no!" I said and forcefully separated them. "Let's go."

As we left the house, we saw Hareton returning from the fields. "I can read now," he said proudly.

"That's brilliant!" Cathy answered. "Show me."

Looking up at the words over the front entrance, he carefully spelt the letters of his own name, struggling over some of them.

"And the numbers?" Cathy encouraged him.

"I don't know those yet," he admitted shyly.

"Oh, you silly thing!" she said, laughing at his failure. I slapped her hand, warning her to stop, but she carried on.

Hareton had been smiling – ready to share in the joke – but the smile soon turned to a **frown**, when he realised she was laughing at him, not with him.

Then, from inside, we heard a laugh. Linton had opened the window to be able to hear our conversation.

Hareton strode into the house, seized Linton's arm and pulled him off the chair, sending him crashing to the floor. Linton screamed.

Hareton disappeared into the courtyard in tears, immediately regretting what he'd done.

We rushed inside and lifted Linton back onto the chair.

But when Cathy tried to hug him, he pushed her away. "That was *your* fault!" he cried "You teased him first!"

They argued for a while but soon Linton declared he was tired, so we said goodbye and left.

That evening, I confessed to my master that we'd been to Wuthering Heights. He forbade Cathy from returning but said she could invite Linton to Thrushcross Grange.

* * * * *

"These things happened last winter, sir," said Mrs Dean, "and now here I am, telling them to you – a stranger to the family! But who knows how much longer you'll be a stranger. You're too young to live long by yourself. And I've noticed you always look very interested whenever I speak of Catherine Linton. Perhaps you love her."

"Stop, Mrs Dean!" I cried. "Maybe I could love her, but would she love me? And anyway, this isn't my home. I belong to the busy world of the city and I'll have to go back to it. Carry on with your story. Did Catherine obey her father?"

* * * * *

She did (the housekeeper replied). She still loved him more than anyone, and he was devoted to her. But he never forgot his wife and often wished to be with her again, lying by her side under the ground.

Spring arrived, but my master's health didn't improve. Linton never visited, as his father had forbidden him from coming.

Although I assured Edgar I'd never abandon Cathy, he grew anxious that his death would leave his daughter alone in the world. Linton was far from the ideal future husband, but if Cathy married her father's heir, at least she'd keep her ancestral home.

Edgar had no idea that Linton's health was as bad as his own. No one did. No doctor ever visited Wuthering Heights and no one saw Linton. I couldn't imagine a father treating his child as tyrannically as Heathcliff treated him, although I only found out about that afterwards.

The closer the child got to death, the more desperate Heathcliff became. He was determined that his son mustn't die before he'd carried out his plans.

Chapter 16

Summer was half over before Edgar reluctantly agreed that his daughter could meet Linton on the moors, halfway between the two houses, if I accompanied her. Cathy and I set out on our first ride to join her cousin. In the end, we met him barely a quarter of a mile from his own door. He'd sent a message to say he preferred that location.

He lay on the ground, waiting for us. He got up to greet us but I immediately noticed he looked really ill.

Cathy had been excited to meet him but her face went pale when she saw him. He leant on her arm weakly, for support.

"I'm better, much better," he insisted, while struggling to breathe, his large blue eyes wandering anxiously all over the place.

Cathy looked at him, concerned. "But you're so gaunt and—"

"I'm tired," he interrupted hurriedly. "It's too hot for walking. Let's rest here."

We sat down but the meeting still didn't go any better. Linton lacked interest in anything Cathy talked about and she couldn't hide her disappointment. He had altered considerably. He used to be spoilt and demanding – now, he hardly noticed we were there and he no longer sought Cathy's attention.

This made Cathy sassy, complaining that, as he obviously wasn't enjoying her company, we would leave immediately.

Unexpectedly, this idea gave him new energy. Glancing towards Wuthering Heights with a terrified look in his eye, he begged Cathy to stay another half an hour, at least.

"I'm not *very* unwell, Cathy," he insisted. "If you see my father, don't tell him I was quiet. He'll be angry."

"I don't care if he gets angry with me," said Cathy proudly.

"No, he'll be angry with *me*," said her cousin, trembling. "Don't make him angry, Cathy. He's very harsh with me."

It became clear that seeing us was just a task for Linton, set for him by his father.

Linton soon dozed off but we stayed, not wanting to leave him alone on the moors.

"I won't come again," Cathy whispered. "I won't come just to please Mr Heathcliff! I'm glad Linton's in better health but he's much less pleasant than he was and less affectionate towards me."

"You think he's in better health?" I asked.

"Yes," she answered, "because before, he complained constantly about how ill he was."

"I disagree, Miss Cathy," I remarked. "I think his health is much worse."

At that moment, we saw Heathcliff coming so we rushed home. I didn't confess the truth about Linton's state to my master because I didn't want to worry him.

Seven days passed and, every day, Edgar's health deteriorated. Cathy's sensitive heart didn't fail to notice and, from that moment, she barely left his side. His bedroom became her whole world.

At last, her father insisted that she go outside for some fresh air. "Why don't you meet Linton again?" he suggested. I knew he was encouraging their relationship so she wouldn't be entirely alone after his death.

We delayed our trip until the afternoon, a golden August afternoon. Every breath from the hills was so full of life that it seemed whoever breathed it, even if they were dying, might recover.

We found Linton in the same spot as last time. He welcomed us with more energy than before but it seemed to come from fear rather than joy.

"It's late. I thought you'd never come," he complained,

breathing loudly and with difficulty, as if he were slowly suffocating.

"My father's very ill," Cathy replied impatiently, "and why have I left his side? I can tell you're no more pleased to see me than last time. Stop clinging to my dress like that! I'm going home!"

"I haven't told you the whole truth," sobbed Linton, "but please, don't leave. He'll kill me! Cathy, my life is in your hands. Please, don't leave!"

Seeing his **distress**, sweet, kind Cathy felt sorry for him and bent down to lift him up. "Tell me the truth then!" she cried. "You wouldn't let an enemy hurt me, would you? Are you that much of a coward?"

"But my father threatens me all the time," gasped the boy. "I'm so scared of him! I can't tell you the truth!"

I listened in silence, determined that I'd never allow anyone to harm my Cathy, when I looked up and saw Heathcliff approaching me.

When he reached me, he said quietly, "I hear Edgar Linton is dying. Is it true?"

"Yes," I replied sadly.

"I want my boy to get his inheritance," he said, glancing at his son two metres away, "so I'd be grateful if Edgar hurried up and died. If Linton dies first, I'll never get

Thrushcross Grange."

I didn't respond.

He now approached Linton but the boy started trembling. "Cathy," Heathcliff said, "please take the worthless brat inside. You can see he won't let me near him – you would think I was the devil or something!"

Cathy started walking towards Wuthering Heights with Linton clinging to her. I tried to stop her, but she wouldn't listen. I walked with them and stopped at the entrance as Cathy took Linton to a chair. Heathcliff, pushing me forward, said, "Come inside too, Nelly. I'm feeling sociable today!"

He shut the door behind me and locked it. I was shocked.

"I'll get you some tea in a minute," he said to me and to Cathy, "but I have something else to offer as well. I mean Linton."

Cathy just stared at him.

"Are you afraid?" he continued, sneering. Then he hit the table with his fist. "I **despise** both of you, you and my idiot son!"

"I'm not afraid of you!" Cathy declared, her black eyes flashing. She approached him, and said, "Give me the key."

Heathcliff, the key in his hand, looked up, surprised at her lack of fear. It is likely that her confidence as well as her appearance also reminded him of the person she'd inherited them from.

She tried to grab the key but Heathcliff, recovered from his surprise, slapped her across the face several times.

I rushed at him furiously, but he hit me on the chest and I fell backwards, nearly suffocating.

Cathy's eyes widened with shock. A moment ago, she had been without fear – now, she trembled, her breath unsteady.

"Go and sit with Linton," Heathcliff ordered her. "He'll be your husband soon so he can comfort you."

But Cathy ran to me instead of her cousin, who didn't look interested in comforting anyone. He only looked relieved that his father hadn't hit *him* for a change.

When Heathcliff left the room, we tried to escape but the windows were too narrow for even Cathy's slim figure.

"Tell us what's going on, Linton," Cathy insisted sternly.

"Father wants us to be married," he finally admitted. "He knows your father wouldn't let us marry yet, and he's afraid that I'll die if we wait. So we're getting married in the morning, and you'll have to stay here tonight. If you do what he wants, you can go home the next day and take me with you."

"Marry you?" I cried. "The man is mad! Why would a beautiful, healthy young lady want to marry a pathetic, selfish boy like you? And you're dishonest too – you tricked us!"

I grabbed him by the shoulders and shook him, but he started coughing so I stopped.

Heathcliff came back into the room and let Linton pass out through the door.

Cathy approached Heathcliff. "I can't stay here!" she cried in distress. "My father won't know where we are! He'll be so worried!"

"Ah, now I'm really determined to keep you here!" said the beast. "I'll enjoy this even more if it's going to make your father miserable. Oh and, by the way, three servants came from Thrushcross Grange just now, looking for you, but I sent them away. I won't let them take you – you'll both remain prisoners here until you and Linton are married."

On finding out that we'd missed our chance to escape, we couldn't control our grief anymore. We cried and cried until we were sent up to bed at nine o'clock.

At seven the next morning, Heathcliff came to collect Cathy but left me in the bedroom. "I'll send your breakfast up in a while," he told me.

There I remained, locked up, for five night and five days,

seeing nobody but Hareton, who brought me food and water without speaking a word to me.

Chapter 17

On the fifth day, a lighter step approached and, this time, Zillah entered the room. "Oh, Mrs Dean, you're safe! I heard you got lost on the moor and that Mr Heathcliff has been looking after you here. Everyone in the village is talking about it."

I told her this was a lie but she didn't believe me.

"I've come to let you out," she explained. "My master's letting you go."

Happy to hear this, I rushed downstairs, looking for Cathy. I found nobody until a slight cough drew my attention to the fireplace. It was Linton.

"Where's Miss Cathy?" I asked him sternly.

"She's upstairs. She's upset because she wants to leave but we won't let her. Father says it's terrible my wife wants to abandon me. She should be happy to be with me but instead she just keeps crying."

"Why aren't you with her if she's upset?" I asked, appalled at his selfishness. "She's always been so patient with you and so caring."

"I can't bear her crying," he whined. "She won't stop.

And she looks so pale and wild that I'm afraid of her."

"Where's your father?" I asked.

"He's in the courtyard talking to the doctor," he replied. "He says Uncle's dying at last. I'm glad because I'll be the master of Thrushcross Grange after him. Cathy always calls it *her* house but it isn't hers! It's mine! Father says everything she has is mine."

I left then and immediately sent four men back to Wuthering Heights to rescue Cathy. But they returned without her. Heathcliff had told them she was ill and couldn't be moved.

Early that evening, as I was fetching a jug of water, I heard a knock at the door. I opened it and someone flew into my arms. It was Cathy! "Is Father still alive?" she asked, sobbing.

I assured her that he was but he wouldn't be with us for much longer. She ran straight up to see him and I left them alone for a quarter of an hour. When I finally joined them, Cathy was supporting her father's head and he was gazing up at her lovingly. She was distressed as she looked back at him, but he was calm. "I'm going to her," he said, "and you, darling child, will join us one day." Then he died peacefully.

Edgar was buried next to his wife, in the quiet little churchyard.

Cathy later explained to me that, as Linton had opened the bedroom door, she'd pushed past him and run around the house, looking for a possible exit. She didn't want to go downstairs because the dogs would start barking and warn Heathcliff that she was escaping. So instead, she ran into her mother's old room, squeezed through the window and, with the help of the fir tree growing against the house, climbed to the ground.

The evening after the funeral, my young lady and I were seated in the sitting room, our minds on our recent loss.

Without any warning and without knocking, Heathcliff strode into the room. He was master here now, after all.

It was the same room he'd entered as a guest eighteen years earlier and the same moon shone through the window. Although we hadn't yet lit a candle, the portraits of Mr and Mrs Linton were clearly visible on the wall.

Cathy tried to run out of the room but Heathcliff seized her arm. "Stop!" he shouted. "No more running away! I've come to take you home."

Cathy was shocked by this idea.

"Why not let Miss Cathy stay here," I begged, "and send Mr Linton to join her? As you hate them both, you wouldn't miss them, surely."

"I'm looking for a tenant for Thrushcross Grange," he

answered. "Right, let's go, Cathy. Hurry up."

"Alright, I'll go with you," said Cathy proudly. "Linton is all I've got to love in the world and you won't make us hate each other."

"I wouldn't be so sure about that," Heathcliff sneered, his lips curling into a cruel smile. "He's angry with you for leaving him. I heard him tell Zillah what he'd do to you if he were as strong as I am. He's very similar to me, you see – he just lacks the strength to carry out his ideas."

"I know he has a bad nature," said Cathy. "He's your son after all. But I have a better nature so I can forgive his. I'll cry for him when he dies, but who will cry for you? You're as lonely as the devil, aren't you, Mr Heathcliff, and jealous like him? Nobody loves you. I wouldn't want to be you!"

Cathy seemed to have decided that, if she had to go and live with Heathcliff at Wuthering Heights, she must be tough, even if that meant taking pleasure in her enemy's suffering.

"You'll soon be sorry to be yourself," said her father-in-law. "Now get your things and come with me!"

In her absence, I begged for Zillah's place at Wuthering Heights, suggesting she could replace me here. But he told me to be silent.

Then he smiled and said, "I'll tell you what I did

yesterday: I asked the man who was digging Edgar's grave to remove the earth from her **coffin** lid, and I opened it. Her face is still the same. I didn't want to leave her but I knew I had to. I broke open one side of the coffin – not the side next to Edgar's coffin, damn him, but the other side. And when I'm dead, my coffin will be put next to hers so we'll always lie beside each other."

"Weren't you ashamed to disturb the dead, Mr Heathcliff?" I cried, astonished.

"Disturb her?" he replied. "She's disturbed me night and day for eighteen years – until last night. Last night, I was peaceful. I dreamt I was sleeping the last sleep by her side, with my heart stopped and my cheek frozen against hers."

Heathcliff paused and wiped his forehead. His hair clung to it, wet with sweat, and his eyes were fixed on the fire.

After a minute, he reached up to Mrs Linton's portrait and took it down, announcing, "I'm taking this to Wuthering Heights."

Cathy came back into the room to tell us that she and her horse were ready.

"You're not bringing your horse," Heathcliff said. "I won't pay someone to look after it. Whatever journeys you take in the future, you can go on foot. Come on."

"Bye, Nelly!" whispered my dear little mistress, her

voice full of emotion. As she kissed me, her lips felt like ice. "Come and see me. Don't forget."

"You'll do no such thing!" Heathcliff shouted at me. "When I wish to speak to you, I'll come here."

I went to the window and watched them leave, Cathy looking back at me with an expression that broke my heart. Heathcliff held her arm tightly and strode off with her, the trees soon hiding them.

Chapter 18

I haven't seen my Cathy since she left. I paid a visit to Wuthering Heights, but Joseph refused to let me in, holding the door tightly. Zillah has kept me updated to some extent, otherwise I'd hardly know who was dead and alive. From the way she talks about Cathy, I can guess she dislikes her – she finds her sassy.

My young lady asked her for help when she first arrived but Heathcliff told Zillah to let his daughter-in-law look after herself, and Zillah happily agreed. She's a selfish woman.

One day, about six weeks ago, I had a long talk with Zillah when we met on the moor. It was just before you arrived. This is what she told me.

"The first thing Mrs Linton did," she said, "after arriving at Wuthering Heights, was to run upstairs, without even wishing me and Joseph good evening. She stayed in Linton's room until morning. Then, while the master and Hareton were having breakfast, she came downstairs and, all panicked, asked for the doctor. Her husband was very ill, she said.

"'We know that!' answered Heathcliff impatiently. 'But his life isn't worth a penny, and I won't spend a penny on him.'

"'But I don't know what to do,' she cried; 'and if nobody will help me, he'll die!'

"'Get out of this room,' growled the master, his tone harsh. 'I don't want to hear another word about him! No one here cares what happens him. If you do, be his nurse. If you don't, lock him in the room and leave him.'

"Then she began to bother me, and I said I'd already had enough trouble with the whining thing. We each had our tasks, and hers was to look after Linton.

"I don't know how they managed together, but I suspect he complained constantly and she didn't get much rest. I could tell that by her white face and heavy eyes. Sometimes, I felt tempted to help her and I didn't think it was right not to call for the doctor, but I had to obey the master, Mrs Dean. Once or twice, at bedtime, I've opened my door and seen her sitting crying at the top of the stairs. I do feel sorry for her then but I don't want to lose my job, you know.

"At last, one night, she woke us all up, crying, 'He's dying – I'm sure of it this time!'

"Mr Heathcliff lit a candle and followed her to their room. He went up to Linton and held the light in his face.

He was dead.

"Hareton and Joseph joined us in the room. Hareton was more interested in staring at Cathy than thinking of Linton. Mr Heathcliff told him to leave the room at once and ordered Joseph to remove the body."

Cathy stayed in her room for a fortnight, according to Zillah. Heathcliff went up once, to show her Linton's will. He'd left all his property, including what had been hers, to his father. Of course, Heathcliff had forced his son to write his will that way.

"One Sunday," Zillah continued, "she asked to come down because her room was so cold. As Mr Heathcliff had gone to Thrushcross Grange and Joseph was at church, I said she could. She was dressed all in black with her yellow curls combed back behind her ears.

"She joined me and Hareton in the kitchen. Hareton was shy with her and very **sullen**, but he couldn't resist checking his hands and clothes to make sure they were clean.

"I laughed at him for that!" Zillah went on. Seeing that I wasn't pleased with what she was telling me, she added, "Mrs Dean, I know you think your young lady is too sophisticated for Hareton, and maybe you're right. She certainly thinks she's superior to all of us. But she isn't – not anymore. She's as poor as you or me now.

"She refused to talk to us and tried to get some books from a shelf so she could sit and read by the fire. She couldn't reach them, though, and Hareton stood up to get them for her. I was convinced she'd reject his offer of help but she didn't, and I could tell Hareton was really pleased. She didn't thank him, though, the spoilt little princess.

"'Will you please read to us?' Hareton asked her kindly, his voice almost a whisper.

"'No!' she shouted, her eyes flashing. 'You two left me alone when I needed you so why should I do anything for you now?'

"'Go to hell, then!' Hareton shouted at her in reply. But from that day, she came downstairs more and more, despite her pride, because she was so lonely upstairs."

I was distressed to hear Zillah's account, but unfortunately there's nothing I can do. The only solution is for her to marry again.

* * * * *

That was the end of Mrs Dean's story. My health is improving rapidly so, although it's only the second week in January, I decided to ride over to Wuthering Heights and inform my landlord that I'm going to spend the next six months in London. He can look for another tenant if he wishes. There's no way I'm spending another winter in this place.

When I arrived, Miss Cathy was there, preparing vegetables for lunch. She didn't greet me or even look up. She was more sulky and even less welcoming than the last time I'd seen her.

"How's Nelly?" she asked me at last.

I assured her Mrs Dean was fine.

"I'm so bored here!" she sighed. "Do you know, I don't even have any books to read! Heathcliff has taken them all away because he doesn't like reading. I found some one day in Hareton's room. Why on earth did you take them, Hareton?" she asked, turning to her cousin. "They're no use to you so why do you hide them and prevent me from enjoying them?"

"Mr Hareton wants to expand his knowledge," I said in his defence. "He'll be a top student in a few years."

"I don't know why he bothers," she laughed. "I heard him reading from one of the books and he was struggling so much, it was really funny."

I could tell the young man was annoyed that she laughed at him for not being able to read and then laughed at him when he tried to learn! And I agreed with him. "We all struggled to start with, Mrs Heathcliff," I remarked.

Hareton sat in silence, looking extremely sullen. Then he

got up and strode out of the room, returning a few minutes later with half a dozen books, which he flung into Cathy's lap. "Take them! I never want to read them again!"

She opened one and started reading it in the way she'd heard him read, copying him and laughing to herself. He swore at her, grabbed the books and flung them in the fire. He'd been teaching himself to read in an effort to seek her approval but, if she was going to tease him, he wouldn't bother anymore.

Heathcliff came home and we had lunch together. He was disappointed I was leaving because it's not easy finding tenants in that remote spot.

As I rode back to Thrushcross Grange later, I thought, "What a miserable life for the members of that household! How romantic it would have been if Cathy and I had got together, as Mrs Dean wanted, and moved to London."

Chapter 19

1802. This September, I was invited to stay with a friend who lives on the moors, and on my journey to his house, I unexpectedly came within fifteen miles of Gimmerton. I was seized by a sudden desire to see Thrushcross Grange again. Three hours later, I was there.

The weather was lovely and warm but as I rode into the valley, I saw that the grey church looked greyer and the lonely churchyard lonelier than before.

I reached Thrushcross Grange before sunset and knocked on the door. A simple servant girl answered, and I asked her if I could come in and see Mrs Dean.

"Mrs Dean?" she repeated, bewildered. "But she lives at Wuthering Heights."

"Can I stay here tonight?" I asked her. "I'll pay, of course."

She panicked because she hadn't expected anyone and the place wasn't ready to receive guests, but she was reassured when I told her she'd have plenty of time to prepare the rooms: I was going for a walk to Wuthering Heights.

I was going to ask her why Mrs Dean had left Thrushcross Grange but she'd disappeared.

A beautiful moon was rising over the hills as I walked to Heathcliff's home. When I arrived, the smell of flowers reached my nose. The doors and windows were wide open.

I could hear the inhabitants before I entered, and felt both curiosity and envy.

"Con-*trary*!" said a voice as sweet as ripe fruit. "That's the third time, you silly thing! I'm not going to tell you again. Remember it or I'll pull your hair!"

"Contrary, then," answered another voice that was deep but soft. "And now kiss me for being such a good pupil."

"No. Read it over correctly first, without a single mistake."

The male speaker began to read. He was a young man, respectably dressed and seated at a table, with a book in front of him. His handsome features **glowed** with pleasure, and his eyes kept moving impatiently from the page to a small white hand over his shoulder. This hand, however, gave him a hard slap on the cheek whenever its owner noticed he wasn't paying attention.

She stood over him, watching him. What a face! I was annoyed at myself for throwing away the chance of doing more than just staring at its beauty.

The task was done and the pupil claimed his reward, receiving at last five kisses on his handsome face. Then they came to the door and, from their conversation, I realised they were about to set off for a walk on the moors.

I didn't interrupt them but instead walked round to the kitchen door at the back. There, I found my old friend, Nelly Dean, sewing and singing a song.

"I'd rather hear swearing in my ears all day than listen to your nonsense!" shouted a voice from the kitchen in a strong Yorkshire accent.

"Read your Bible, old man, and never mind me," replied the singer.

Mrs Dean was about to restart her song when I approached her. She jumped to her feet and welcomed me warmly.

"What are you doing here?" I asked her.

"Zillah left and Mr Heathcliff asked me to come back here, soon after you went to London."

"Is your master here?" I asked.

"He's gone out," she said. "But anyway, it's Mrs Heathcliff you should deal with."

I looked surprised.

"Ah! You didn't know Heathcliff had died, I see."

"Heathcliff is dead?" I declared, astonished. "When did

he die?"

"Three months ago. But sit down and I'll tell you all about it."

She went to get me a drink and I heard Joseph mumbling that she should be embarrassed having a boyfriend at her age.

* * * * *

I was ordered to come to Wuthering Heights, as I said (she began), and I obeyed happily because I was dying to see Cathy again. The first time I saw her I was deeply shocked. She'd altered so much since our separation.

She spent a lot of time with me in the kitchen and Hareton would often join us, occupied with some task. Initially, she ignored him, and he was sullen and miserable. But slowly, her behaviour changed and soon, she wouldn't leave him alone, chatting to him and teasing him about how simple and stupid he was.

"Hareton will ask the master to send you upstairs, if you don't behave!" I said. I could see Hareton's fist lay ready in his lap, as if he were tempted to use it against her.

"I know why Hareton never speaks when I'm in the kitchen," she cried, on another occasion. "He's afraid I'll laugh at him. Nelly, what do you think?"

"I think you're very rude to him," I answered sternly.

"Perhaps I am," she went on, "but he's so silly. Hareton, if I gave you a book, would you take it now? Come on."

She placed one in front of him but he flung it away and muttered that if she didn't leave him alone, he'd break her neck.

I could see she felt bad now for putting him off learning to read. But she was clever and soon came up with a plan. She would start reading aloud to me while I worked and stop at an interesting part. Then she'd leave the book open on the table, hoping he would pick it up and read it once she'd gone. But he was too stubborn for that.

One day, she approached him and said, rather shyly, "Hareton, I want—I mean, I would like you to be my cousin now, if you hadn't grown so angry and rough with me."

Hareton gave no answer.

"Hareton, Hareton, Hareton! Do you hear me?" she cried.

"Go away!" he growled, gruffly.

"I won't let you ignore me anymore!" she cried, in a determined voice.

"I'll go to hell, body and soul," he answered, "before I look at you again."

Cathy frowned and went back to sit by the window.

"You should be friends with your cousin, Hareton," I

interrupted, "since she regrets how rude she was. It would do you a great deal of good to have her as a companion."

"A companion!" he cried. "When she hates me and doesn't think I'm good enough to clean her shoes?"

"I don't hate you. You hate *me*!" sobbed Cathy, no longer hiding her feelings. "You hate me as much as Heathcliff does, and more."

"You're a damn liar," began Hareton. "If I hate you so much, why have I made him angry by taking your side a hundred times? And I did that even when you sneered at me and despised me. Just leave me alone!"

"I didn't know you took my side," she answered, surprised. She dried her eyes and looked at him, her gaze soft. "But thank you. I was so miserable and bitter at everybody that I didn't realise. Will you forgive me?"

She went up to him and put out her hand but he wouldn't take it. He just stared at the ground, his face as black as a thundercloud. But Cathy realised he was being stubborn and that he didn't really despise her so she bent down and gave him a gentle kiss on the cheek. Then she went and sat back down in her chair.

I looked at her disapprovingly but she just said, "Well, he wouldn't shake hands with me. And I want to be friends."

Hareton, meanwhile, was careful not to show his face for

a minute or two and he certainly didn't dare even glance at Cathy.

Five minutes later, Cathy came to me with a book, neatly wrapped in white paper. She'd written "Mr Hareton Earnshaw" on it and asked me to pass it to him. "And tell him, if he'll take it, I'll teach him to read it."

Hareton wouldn't take it so I placed it in his lap. I watched him, not breathing, fully expecting him to throw it to the ground. But he didn't. Cathy stayed in her seat, her back turned, until she heard him removing the paper. Then she quietly got up and moved to sit next to her cousin. He trembled and his face glowed.

"Say you forgive me, Hareton."

He muttered something.

"And you'll be my friend?" she added.

"No. You'll be ashamed of me every day of your life," he answered, "and I can't bear it."

"So you won't be my friend?" she said, moving closer to him, her smile as sweet as honey.

I couldn't hear any more of their conversation but when I looked round again, I saw two such cheerful faces, leaning over the book, that I knew they were no longer enemies.

When it was time for bed, Cathy went upstairs singing.

Their relationship developed rapidly. It didn't always go

perfectly – Hareton was still often rough and my young lady isn't a patient person. But they shared a common goal – one loving and wanting to respect, the other loving and wanting to be respected – and, in the end, they achieved it.

You see, Mr Lockwood, it was easy enough to win Mrs Heathcliff's heart. But now, I'm glad you didn't try. I won't envy anyone on their wedding day: there won't be a happier woman than me in the whole of England!

Chapter 20

The following day, Cathy went downstairs before me and by the time I joined her, I saw she'd persuaded Hareton to clear the fruit bushes from a large area of ground. They were busy planning to bring some plants over from Thrushcross Grange to replace them.

I was shocked by the destruction that had been achieved in a brief thirty minutes and I told them so. The bushes had been Joseph's delight and she wanted to put a flower **bed** there instead.

"I'd forgotten they were Joseph's," answered Earnshaw, rather embarrassed.

We always ate our meals with Heathcliff. As we entered the room that morning, I quietly warned Cathy not to make her new friendship with Hareton obvious to the master because he'd be annoyed with them both.

But she didn't take any notice. After only one minute, she moved slowly towards him and put a flower on his plate.

He hardly dared look at her but she kept teasing him and twice he nearly burst into laughter. I frowned and glanced towards the master. I could see, however, that his mind was elsewhere. But soon, Cathy started her nonsense again and, at last, Hareton laughed loudly.

Heathcliff looked up, surprised, his eyes moving to our faces. Cathy looked straight at him bravely.

"Don't stare back at me with those devil's eyes of yours! And shut up. I don't want to hear your laughing."

"It was me," muttered Hareton.

"What did you say?" asked the master.

Hareton fixed his eyes on his plate and didn't repeat the confession. Heathcliff looked at him for a while and then silently returned to his breakfast, soon lost in his own thoughts again.

The two young people moved apart and I thought we'd have no more drama, but then Joseph appeared at the door, with trembling lips and furious eyes.

He shouted something but we could barely understand him in his anger.

"Oh, what is it, you idiot?" cried Heathcliff impatiently. "I don't care what Nelly's done."

"It's not Nelly!" answered Joseph. And then he mumbled something again.

"Are you drunk?" Heathcliff said angrily.

"I've pulled up two or three bushes," Hareton admitted.

"Why have you done that?" asked the master.

"We wanted to plant some flowers there," Cathy said.

"And who the hell gave *you* permission to touch a stick in my garden?" asked her father-in-law, astonished. "And who ordered *you* to obey her?" he added, turning to Hareton.

"Why shouldn't I decorate a small part of the garden when you've taken all my land?" cried Cathy.

"You never had any, you stupid girl!" answered Heathcliff.

"And you took my money," she continued, glaring back at him.

"Shut up!" he shouted.

"And you took Hareton's land and his money!" the careless thing went on. "Hareton and I are friends now and I'm going to tell him all about you!"

"Get her out of my sight, Nelly, or I'll kill her!" Heathcliff warned savagely, but we were all too shocked to move.

His black eyes flashed and he got up, approaching Cathy and grabbing her hair. Hareton tried to stop him, begging him not to hurt her. I got up to help rescue her but suddenly, Heathcliff froze. He gazed at her face, then covered his own with his hand and stood for a moment, calming himself.

"Go with Nelly, both of you, and stay with her," he said.

"Get out!"

We saw each other again at lunchtime, then Heathcliff went out, saying he wouldn't be back before evening.

While he was gone, the two new friends started chatting. They were soon arguing, however, Cathy criticising Heathcliff's recent behaviour. Hareton warned her that he wouldn't listen to her talk about the older man like that. "How would you like it if I started criticising your father?" he asked.

She showed a good heart and, from that time, she never once spoke against Heathcliff in Hareton's presence again.

With this slight disagreement over, they were friends again, and became once more pupil and teacher. I enjoyed watching them. They both felt like my children, in a way, you know, even though he was twenty-one by now and she eighteen. His honest, warm and intelligent nature soon shone through his earlier degradation. And as his mind brightened, his features brightened too.

While I was admiring them, the master returned. They lifted their eyes together and both looked straight at him. Perhaps you've never noticed but their eyes are very similar, and they are those of Catherine Earnshaw. I suppose this similarity took Heathcliff by surprise.

He walked up to the pair and picked up the book. Then

he returned it without saying anything. The two young people left the room after this but Heathcliff asked me to stay.

"I wanted to seek revenge but look what's happened," he remarked, having sat in silence for a while, thinking about the scene he'd just witnessed. "My old enemies haven't beaten me, and I could still punish their children. Who would stop me? But what's the use? I don't care about revenge anymore. I can't even be bothered to raise my hand! I've lost the ability to enjoy their destruction, and I don't have the energy to destroy for nothing."

There was a strange look in his eyes as he continued. "Nelly, there's a change approaching and I'm in its shadow. I take so little interest in my daily life that I hardly remember to eat and drink. Looking at those two reminds me of *her*! It's painful! But then, what is *not* connected to her for me? I can't look at this floor without seeing her face in it. She's in every cloud, in every tree; she fills the night air. I'm surrounded by her image! The entire world is a collection of things that remind me that she existed and I lost her!"

"But what do you mean by a *change*, Mr Heathcliff?" I said, made uneasy by his manner. He didn't seem in danger of dying, though – he still looked strong and healthy. And apart from an obsession with his lost love, he wasn't crazy at all.

"I don't know, but I know that I can't carry on like this. I have to remind myself to breathe, almost to remind my heart to beat. I have a single wish, one that has become my whole life. Oh God, it's a long fight. I wish it were over!"

He began to walk around the room, muttering terrible things to himself, till I began to believe that earth had become a hell to him. I wondered how it would end.

Chapter 21

For a few days after that evening, Heathcliff didn't eat with us. He only had one meal a day, alone.

One night, after the family were in bed, I heard him go downstairs and out the front door. I didn't hear him come back in, and in the morning, I found he was still away.

It was April then, and the weather was mild and pleasant. After breakfast, Cathy insisted that I bring a chair and sit with my sewing under the fir trees at the end of the house. Hareton was busy digging and arranging her little flower bed, which they'd moved to that new spot following Joseph's complaints.

Suddenly, Cathy, who had run down to the gate to pick some flowers for the garden, rushed to tell us that Heathcliff was coming. She seemed confused. "He looked so different to normal that I stopped for a moment to stare at him."

"In what way?" asked Hareton, immediately worried.

"Almost bright and cheerful. No, not *almost*. *Very* excited, and wild, and glad!" she replied.

"Wandering around at night amuses him, then," I remarked, trying to sound unconcerned while actually feeling anxious. Seeing the master looking glad was not an everyday sight.

As he walked into the house, I followed him. He was pale and trembling but, yes, there was certainly a joyful glow in his eyes, which altered the appearance of his whole face.

"Will you have some breakfast?" I said.

"No, I'm not hungry," he answered, looking away.

"You shouldn't stay out all night," I told him. "It's still damp at this time of year. You'll catch a cold."

"Don't annoy me," he replied.

I obeyed and, as I walked past him, I noticed he was breathing as fast as a cat. "Yes, he's ill," I thought.

Later, he came in to lunch but, as he was about to start eating, he got up, walked to the window then left the room.

After an hour or two, he came back in but he was no calmer – he had the same unnatural (it *was* unnatural) appearance of joy under his eyebrows. His whole body was shivering.

I watched him, worried. I hesitated to question him but, finally, I asked, "Where were you last night?"

"You're very curious, Nelly!" he laughed. "I should say it's none of your business but I'll answer you. Last night, I was at the gate of hell. Today, I'm within sight of my heaven. You'd better go."

I wiped the table and left.

I didn't see him again that day. At dinner time, I carried his food to him on a tray. He was leaning on the window ledge and the room was filled with the damp air of the evening.

He didn't seem to notice me. "Shall I close the window?" I asked him.

The light from my candle flashed on his features as I spoke. Oh, Mr Lockwood, I can't express what a terrible shock I got from the sight. Those deep, dark eyes! That strange smile and ghostly paleness. It appeared to me not Mr Heathcliff but a supernatural creature. In my terror, I moved back and the candle touched the wall, going out and leaving me in darkness.

"Yes, close it," he replied, in his familiar voice.

I did what he said before rushing out in fear.

I heard him go upstairs soon afterwards, but he didn't go into his own bedroom – he went into the bedroom with the writing scratched into the window ledge. Its window is wide enough to climb out of and I suspected he was planning another midnight excursion.

But, in fact, he didn't leave the room. Instead, he walked backwards and forwards for hours, muttering. The only word I could catch was Catherine's name, spoken as though he were talking to someone present and from the depth of his soul.

"Is he a vampire?" I wondered. I'd read of such terrible creatures. But then I remembered that I'd known him since he was little and followed him through almost his whole life, and I shouldn't think such silly nonsense.

"But where did he come from, that little dark thing, taken in by a good man only to bring him trouble?" muttered my **superstitious** mind, as I dozed off. While I slept, I had strange dreams, imagining who his parents were and even seeing his death and funeral. We didn't know his full name or his age so his **headstone** only had the single word, "Heathcliff". That came true. If you visit the churchyard, you'll read, on his headstone, only that and the date of his death.

With the dawn, my common sense returned. When I went downstairs to prepare the breakfast, Heathcliff was discussing some farm business with Joseph, who then left.

Sat at the table, Heathcliff didn't eat or drink anything. He just smiled strangely, not noticing me.

"Mr Heathcliff!" I cried, feeling superstitious again. "For God's sake, don't stare as if you saw a supernatural vision."

He asked if we were alone. I replied that we were – the young pair were eating their breakfast outside under the trees.

"Master, you must eat something!" I cried. "And you must rest."

"Nelly," he replied, "you might as well tell a man struggling in the water to rest when he's within a metre of the shore! I must reach it first, and then I'll rest."

I thought for a moment, then said, "Mr Heathcliff, you've lived a selfish life. Would it hurt you to call for a priest and talk to him? How can you hope to enter heaven otherwise?"

"Thanks for reminding me of the way I want to be buried," he replied. "I don't want a priest or a funeral service. I've nearly reached *my* heaven – other people's 'heaven' is not something I seek or need."

Then, saying he wanted to be alone, he got up and left the house, walking down the garden path and disappearing through the gate. He didn't come home till late and then he went straight to his bedroom.

That evening was very wet, and the rain poured down until dawn. When Heathcliff didn't come down for breakfast, I went upstairs, using my spare key to unlock his door. I went in. The window was open, swinging in the wind. Heathcliff was on the bed, lying on his back. His eyes met mine, so keen and fierce that I started, and then he seemed to smile. I didn't think he was dead, but his face and throat were washed with rain and he was perfectly still.

I touched his hand, which was resting on the window ledge. It was cold. There could be no doubt anymore – he was dead!

I tried to close his eyes but they wouldn't close, seeming to sneer at my attempts.

I called for Joseph. He came straight away but refused to touch the body. "Ah, the devil's carried away his soul," he muttered.

Poor Hareton was the only one who suffered from Heathcliff's death, even though the master had harmed him the most. He finally got his inheritance but he didn't care about it. He stayed by the body all night. He kissed the savage face and cried with a genuine grief, from a heart that was as strong as steel but also very kind.

We buried Heathcliff as he had requested. I hope he's now sleeping peacefully. However, the superstitious country people, if you ask them, would swear on the Bible that he *walks*. Some of them claim to have seen him near the church, on the moors and even within this house. Silly stories, you'll say, Mr Lockwood. Nevertheless, Joseph insists he's seen the two of them looking out of Heathcliff's window on every rainy night since his death.

I don't like being out in the dark now, and I don't like

being left by myself in this bleak place. I'll be glad when the young couple leave it and move to Thrushcross Grange.

* * * * *

"They're moving, then?" I said.

"Yes," answered Mrs Dean, "as soon as they're married, which will be on New Year's Day."

"And who will live here then?"

"Joseph will live in the kitchen and the rest of the house will be shut up."

"For the use of any ghosts who want to live here?" I suggested, smiling slightly.

"No, Mr Lockwood," said Nelly, shaking her head. "I believe the dead are at peace."

At that moment, the garden gate swung shut. The walkers were returning.

"They're not afraid of anything," I said jealously, watching them approach through the window.

As they reached the front door, they stopped and looked up at the moon – or, more precisely, they looked at each other by the light of the moon.

I said good night to Mrs Dean and left Wuthering Heights, walking back to Thrushcross Grange through the churchyard. I looked for, and soon found, the three headstones on the slope by the edge of the moor – the middle one grey and half-buried by grass, Edgar Linton's with some plants growing over it, and Heathcliff's, still bare.

I stood there, gazing at them under that gentle sky, listening to the soft wind breathing through the grass, wondering how anyone could ever imagine anything but peaceful rest for the sleepers in that quiet earth.

THE END

MORE STORIES

A1+ Elementary

A2 Pre-intermediate

B1 Intermediate

B2 Upper intermediate

VISIT MY WEBSITE

You will find:
- information about my other books
- free stories
- free exercises for this book
  (vocabulary exercises, comprehension exercises and notes about British culture)

ReadStories-LearnEnglish.com

Words from the story

appalled (adj)
feeling shocked or horrified by something bad or unpleasant

banister (n)
a handrail at the side of a staircase

beast (n)
a large or dangerous animal, or someone who behaves in a cruel or unpleasant way

bed (n)
a garden plot where flowers are grown

bewildered (adj)
confused and unsure about something

bleak (adj)
cold and dreary; without hope or encouragement

brat (n)
a spoiled or badly behaved child

brighten (v)
make something more cheerful or light

cling (v)
hold onto something tightly, often because of fear or affection (past form, **clung**)

coffin (n)
a box in which a dead person is buried

comfort (v)
make someone feel better when they are sad, worried or upset

courtyard (n)
an open space surrounded by buildings

degradation (n)
the process of treating someone or something badly, leading to a loss of dignity or quality (v, **degrade**)

despise (v)
strongly dislike someone

deterioration (n)
the process of becoming worse or weaker over time
(v, **deteriorate**)

distraught (adj)
extremely upset or worried

distress (n)
great pain or worry

doomed (adj)
certain to fail or suffer in the future

dote on (phr v)
show excessive love or fondness for someone

doze off (phr v)
fall asleep, usually for a short time

dusk (n)
the period of time just after sunset when the sky is partially dark

dwell on (phr v)
keep thinking or talking about something, often in a way that's unnecessary or unhelpful

fireplace (n)
a space in the wall of a room for a fire, typically with a chimney for smoke to escape

fir tree (n)
a type of evergreen tree with needle-like leaves, often used as Christmas trees

fist (n)
a hand with the fingers tightly closed

fling (v)
throw something suddenly and with force

forceful (adj)
having a lot of power or influence

frown (n)
a facial expression showing disapproval or worry (v, **frown**)

gamble (v)
bet money on something that has an uncertain outcome

gasp (v)
take a quick, sharp breath because of surprise, shock or pain

gaunt (adj)
extremely thin, often because of illness or hunger

glare (v)
look at someone or something with an angry or intense stare

glow (v)
shine with a soft, steady light

grasp (v)
hold something tightly

growl (v)
make a low, rumbling sound, often showing anger or aggression

gruff (adj)
having a rough, low and unfriendly voice or manner

grumpy (adj)
in a bad mood, often easily annoyed or upset

harsh (adj)
severe or cruel; unpleasantly rough or strong

headstone (n)
a stone marker placed at the head of a grave

headstrong (adj)
determined to do what one wants, often in a way that is difficult or stubborn

heir (n)
a person who is legally entitled to inherit someone's property

housekeeper (n)
a person employed to manage household tasks, such as cleaning and cooking

how dare you (phr)
a phrase expressing anger or shock at someone's actions

late (adj)
no longer alive

ledge (n)
a narrow horizontal surface, often found at the edge of a window, which can hold objects or provide support

lock (n)
a small, twisted section of hair

locket (n)
a small ornamental necklace, which holds a picture or other small item

long (v)
have a strong desire for something or someone

maiden name (n)
the surname a woman had before she got married

menacing (adj)
threatening harm or danger

moor (n)
a large area of open, uncultivated land, often covered with grass and heather

on earth (idiom)
used for emphasis to question the existence of something or someone

orphan (n)
a child whose parents are dead

out of my sight (phr)
a phrase used to tell someone to leave or go away, often in anger

outcast (n)
a person who is rejected or excluded from a group

puny (adj)
weak or small in size or strength

reassure (v)
make someone feel less worried or uncertain

reluctant (adj)
unwilling or hesitant to do something

reserved (adj)
showing little emotion or interest; keeping personal thoughts private

sassy (adj)
behaving in a bold, confident or cheeky way

savage (adj)
violent, fierce or extremely cruel

settle in (phr v)
become comfortable in a new place or situation

sharp contrast (phr)
a very noticeable difference between two things

sin (n)
an act considered wrong or immoral, especially according to religious beliefs (person, **sinner**)

slap (v)
hit someone with an open hand (n, **slap**)

slovenly (adj)
untidy or careless in appearance

sneer (v)
smile or speak in a way that shows disrespect or dislike

solitude (n)
the state of being alone, often by choice

spoilt (adj)
someone or something that has been ruined or damaged, often by excessive care or attention

start (v)
move suddenly, especially because of surprise or fear

stern (adj)
serious and severe in manner or attitude

stride (v)
walk with long, confident steps

suffocate (v)
stop someone from breathing, often leading to unconsciousness or death

sulk (v)
be silent and upset, often because of disappointment or anger

sullen (adj)
gloomy, sad or silent because of anger or disappointment

superior (adj)
better than others in quality or status; a person of higher rank

superstitious (adj)
believing in things that are not based on science or reason, such as the supernatural or luck

support (v)
help or hold something up, prevent from falling or being damaged

tenant (n)
a person who rents a property

tyrant (n)
a ruler who uses power in a cruel or oppressive way
(adj, **tyrannical**)

twist (v)
turn something in a circular motion, often to change its shape

unruly (adj)
difficult to control or manage

will (n)
a legal document that decides how a person's property is divided after they die

whine (v)
complain in an annoying, crying voice

worthless (adj)
having no value or importance

www.ingramcontent.com/pod-product-compliance
Lightning Source LLC
Chambersburg PA
CBHW011420070526
44584CB00026BA/3781